How to Use Companies to Slash Your Property Taxes

By

James Bailey

Publisher Details
This guide is published by Tax Portal Ltd. PO Box 844, Warrington, WA5 3ZT

'How to Use Companies to Slash Your Property Taxes' – First published in June 2006.

Second Edition April 2007

A CIP Copy of this book is available from the British Library

978-0-9555741-1-5

Disclaimer

1. This guide is produced for General guidance only, and professional advice should be sought before any decision is made. Individual circumstances can vary and therefore no responsibility can be accepted by the author, James Bailey, or the publisher Tax Portal Ltd, for any action taken, or any decision made to refrain from action, by any readers of this guide.

2. Tax rules and legislation are constantly changing and therefore the information printed in this guide is correct at the time of printing – April 2007.

3. Neither the author nor Tax Portal Ltd offer financial, legal or investment advice. If you require such advice then, we urge you to seek the opinion of an appropriate professional in the relevant field. We care about your success and therefore encourage you to take appropriate advice before you put any of your financial or other resources at risk. Don't forget, investment values can decrease as well as increase.

4. To the fullest extent permitted by law, James Bailey and Tax Portal Ltd do not accept liability for any direct, indirect, special, consequential or other losses or damages of whatsoever kind arising from using this guide.

   The guide itself is provided 'as is' without express or implied warranty.

5. James Bailey and Tax Portal Ltd reserve the right to alter any part of this guide any time without notice

Contents

About James Bailey

James Bailey is a freelance Chartered Tax Adviser who specialises in helping accountants and solicitors with their clients' tax affairs.

He advises family businesses and their owners, and other wealthy individuals. He provides advice on tax planning together with help in dealing with tax investigations.

He began his career as an Inspector of Taxes with the Inland Revenue, latterly as the Deputy District Inspector of a large London tax district. He ran investigations into the tax affairs of individuals and companies, ranging from local businesses to national companies and a few well-known media figures!

After leaving the Inland Revenue, he worked with two of the "Big 4" accounting firms, specialising in tax planning for family companies and wealthy individuals. He advised such businesses on how to minimise their tax liabilities, and their owners on how to reduce or eliminate the capital gains tax due when the business was sold.

He also helped the owners of family businesses to pass them on to the next generation without any inheritance tax becoming due. As an ex-Inspector of Taxes, he also dealt with Inland Revenue tax investigations, both at local level and with more serious cases involving the Inland Revenue's Special Compliance Office.

James has appeared on TV and radio to comment on taxation issues, and written articles on tax planning for various professional journals.

James is one of the lead UK Tax Specialists to the www.property-tax-portal.co.uk and www.taxinsider.co.uk websites and regularly writes tax saving articles and provides specialist tax planning advice for property investors.

When James is not busy helping people sort out their tax affairs he enjoys the country life, field sports, and trying to persuade his spaniel and labrador to behave themselves. When the weather is bad (as it often is in Devon where he lives) he reads detective stories and does crosswords.

If you need tax planning advice then you can email James on a professional basis at: james@property-tax-portal.co.uk.

About This Guide

One of the most common questions I get asked is "should I use a limited company or not?"

There is no simple answer to this question, and there is a great deal of myth and misunderstanding about limited companies.

The purpose of this guide is to set out the benefits and drawbacks of using a limited company as a vehicle for a property business, and to compare them with other possible business structures.

Over the last few years, there has been a rush to incorporate (to transfer their business into a limited company) by many small businesses, egged on by the tax breaks introduced by the Chancellor of the Exchequer in 2000 and in 2002. These tax breaks were withdrawn with effect from April 2006, and as a result, the decision whether to incorporate or not has become more difficult, particularly as the 2007 Budget announced increases in the small companies' rate of corporation tax to 20% for 2007, rising to 22% in 2009.

This guide assumes you have no previous knowledge or experience of limited companies. By the time you finish it, I hope you will have a much clearer idea of the way a company works, and whether it is the right vehicle for your business.

1. Choosing the Right Structure

Anyone wishing to run a business in the UK has a wide choice of ways to organise it. Each possible structure has its own advantages and disadvantages.

This chapter gives an overview of the three basic types of business structures that are commonly used.

1.1. Sole Trader

This is the simplest form of business.

A sole trader owns and runs his business directly – he is "self-employed". All the risks and rewards are his directly, and all the decisions about the business are his.

If things go well he owns all the profits he has made (after he has paid tax on them!).

If things go badly, he is liable for all the debts of the business. He has "unlimited liability" – if his business fails, his private property can be taken to pay off the debts of the business.

1.2. Partnership

Where two or more people own and run a business together, they are known as a partnership.

Like a sole trader, all the risks and rewards belong to the partners – but the crucial point is that EACH partner is JOINTLY liable for the partnership's debts.

If things go wrong any money owed by the business can be recovered from the partners – and if one of them has no money to pay, the other partners will have to pay his share of the debts as well. Like the sole trader, a partner's liability is "unlimited".

1.3. Limited Company

A Limited Company is a "legal person". This means that it exists independently of its shareholders, and it can make contracts, and be sued for its debts.

The word "Limited" means that the shareholders' liability is <u>limited</u> to the money they have invested in their shares. If things go wrong, the worst that can happen to the shareholders is that they will not get their money back - though as we shall see, this is not in fact always the case.

1.4. Types of Partnerships

There is really only one kind of sole trader, but there are different kinds of partnership.

The basic type of partnership is defined by the Partnership Act 1890, and involves "persons carrying on a business in common with a view to profit".

A partnership is not a separate legal person from its members, and for tax purposes it is "transparent". In other words, the partnership itself does not pay tax – each partner pays tax on his share of the profits.

In Scotland, a partnership is a legal person, but for tax purposes, it is treated in the same way as an English partnership, and is "transparent" like them.

In some cases, although two people may agree to share the income from a project, they are not strictly a partnership because they are not carrying on "a business in common".

In such a case, the activity is known as a "joint venture".

HM Revenue and Customs (HMRC) will sometimes claim that this is the case where a jointly owned property is rented out, and this can have significant tax consequences, as we shall see later.

We have seen how the partners in a partnership are jointly liable for the business debts.

There are some varieties of partnership where this is not entirely the case and these are detailed in the following sections.

1.4.1. A "Limited Partnership"

A "Limited Partnership" is one where one or more of the partners has his liability limited to the capital he contributes to the partnership when he joins – like a shareholder, the worst that can happen to him is that he loses the money he invested, unlike an ordinary partner who might lose everything.

There are special rules for such partnerships:

- At least one of the partners must be a "general partner" who has unlimited liability as in an ordinary partnership, and is responsible for running the business.
- A limited partner is not allowed to withdraw any of his capital from the partnership until he leaves the firm.
- A limited partner is not allowed to take part in running the partnership's business, or to make contracts etc., on behalf of the firm – if he does, he loses his limited liability and becomes an ordinary partner.
- There are restrictions on how much relief such partners can have for any losses made by the partnership, and they cannot get tax relief for the interest on any money they borrow to invest in the partnership.

Such partnerships are rather specialised entities, but they can have their uses.

Case Study - 1 A "Limited Partnership"

Mary wants to set up a new business, and her Aunt Sally is prepared to invest 60% of the capital needed to help her, in exchange for a fair share of the profits.

She doesn't want to have "unlimited liability" so the obvious solution seems to be a company, but Sally owns another company, and her tax adviser has warned her that if Mary forms a company and Sally has 60% of the shares, the two companies will be "associated" for tax purposes (which we will see later, can be bad news).

Instead, he suggests that the new business is set up as a limited partnership, with Mary as the General Partner and Sally as the Limited Partner.

This way, Sally has limited liability as she would have had with a company, but without the tax problems of having an "associated company".

In other words a limited partner must be a "sleeping partner" – that is, a partner who does not get involved in running the partnership.

1.4.2. A Limited Liability Partnership (known as an LLP)

This is a fairly new sort of business entity, which was made possible by the Limited Liability Partnership Act 2000.

Unlike a normal partnership, it is a separate legal person from its members, but for tax purposes it is "transparent" like an ordinary partnership.

As the name implies, the partners in an LLP have limited liability, like shareholders in a company.

LLPs have proved popular with large professional firms such as accountants and solicitors, but as a general rule they are not appropriate for the smaller property investor or trader, being rather cumbersome to administer.

The idea of LLPs was that they would combine the advantages of a company (limited liability) with those of a partnership (informality and flexibility).

Some would say, however, that they also combine the disadvantages!

Except for unusual situations like Case Study - 1, the most suitable form of partnership for the property investor is likely to be the traditional Partnership Act type, as described above.

2. Getting to Grips with Limited Companies

In this chapter we will start to understand the structure of Limited Companies.

2.1. The Different Types of Limited Company

There are several types of Limited Company:

A Private Limited Company is the type we shall be concentrating on in this guide. It is the basic type of limited company, used by hundreds of thousands of businesses.

A Public Limited Company ("plc") is allowed to raise funds by selling shares to the public, but it is also subject to much stricter legal controls than a Private Limited Company.

A Listed Company is a plc whose shares can be traded on the Stock Exchange.
There are some other types of company, such as a **company limited by guarantee** – this is normally used by charities, and because it is not allowed to distribute its profits to its shareholders, it is ideal for that purpose – and useless for a property investor!

> For the rest of this guide, when I use the word "company" I shall be referring to a **private limited company**.

2.2. The Basic Rules for a Company

The basic rules for a company are:

- It must have at least one shareholder. The shareholders own the company, and their ownership is evidenced by the number of **shares** they own. If, for example, a company has a total of 100 shares issued to its shareholders, someone who owns 51 of those shares owns 51% of the company.

  He also **"controls"** the company, because in normal circumstances he will have 51 out of 100 votes at the company's **Annual General Meeting** (see below).

- It must have at least one director. Directors are responsible for running the company's business affairs. The shareholders own the company, but the directors run it on a day to day basis. In the case of the typical smaller property business company, the directors are often the shareholders as well.

- It must have a Company Secretary. The Company Secretary is responsible for filing returns with Companies House – see below. The Company Secretary can also be a Director, but there must be at least one Director who is not the Company Secretary – in other words, the minimum number of people to run a company is two – a Director and a Company Secretary.

- A company must prepare and file accounts each year with Companies House (the government agency that regulates UK companies). These must be filed within 10 months of the end of the period covered by the accounts.

- A company must also file various returns of other information with Companies House, notifying such things as the issue or transfer of its shares, the appointment of new directors, and so on.

- A Company must have a **Memorandum and Articles of Association.** This is a formal document which sets out the basic structure of the company – the number of shares it can issue, the rules for transferring shares from one person to another, and the purposes for which the company has been formed.

  Although these "Mem & Arts" are available as standard format documents, it is important to be sure that they are appropriate for your particular company.

  If necessary, the "Mem & Arts" can be altered, but there is a formal process for doing this.

- A Company must hold an **Annual General Meeting ("AGM")** of its shareholders, to approve its accounts and to perform various other administrative tasks. Certain events, such as making a change to the company's "Mem & Arts", may require another meeting during the year, known as an **Extraordinary General Meeting ("EGM").**

- Decisions made by the directors or shareholders of a company should be recorded in the company's **Minutes** – which are a formal record of such things as appointing new directors, issuing shares, or paying dividends.

  There is an example of a company **minute** in section 6.4.1 of this guide.

If this sounds a daunting list of tasks, do not despair – there are a number of specialist companies that offer help with these tasks, and your accountant will be able to advise you on compliance with the routine requirements.

Golden Rule

It is important to realise, however, that a company is a more formal structure than a sole trader or a partnership, and that there are penalties for failing to comply with the rules.

The accounts of a company must be prepared according to certain rules and in a certain format. **You will need an accountant to prepare these for you.**

Companies with a turnover of over £5.6million, or assets of more than £2.8million, are also required to have their accounts "audited" – that is, checked for accuracy by an independent accountant.

Even if your company falls below these limits, you should include the cost of having company accounts prepared by an accountant when you look at the figures for your company.

All the above requirements for companies mean that you should budget for at least £1,000 in "compliance" costs for each year – to cover preparation of accounts, submission of the various statutory returns, and working out the tax payable by the company.

This is a minimum figure – but it will be the one I shall use in the case studies which compare companies with other business entities.

Once a company has filed its accounts, they become **public information.**

Anyone (including your employees or your competitors) can pay a small fee to Companies House and get a copy of the accounts, together with information on the shareholders and directors of the company.

For companies that are excused from being audited, only "abbreviated" accounts need be filed and made public – "abbreviated" accounts do not show as much detail as full accounts (for example there is no profit and loss account) but nevertheless, they give quite a lot of information about the company.

3. Understanding Corporation Tax

In this chapter we will understand the meaning of Corporation Tax ("CT") and will look at how this tax affects companies.

3.1. The Rates of Corporation Tax

Companies pay Corporation Tax ("CT") on their profits – including their capital gains. The rates of corporation tax for 2007/08 are as follows:

Profits	Rate of CT
Up to £300,000 (the "small companies rate")	20%
From £300,000 to £1.5million (the "marginal rate")	32.5%
Over £1.5million (on ALL profits) ("the full rate")	30%

This means that a company with profits of £400,000 would pay CT of £92,500, as follows:

Profits	Rate of CT	Tax payable
£0 - £300,000	20%	£60,000
£300,001 - £400,000	32.5%	£32,500
Total	23.13%%	£92,500

So the highest overall rate of CT a company can pay is 30%, and as long as its profits for the year are less than £1.5million, its rate of CT will be lower than this.

3.2. The Effect of Associated Companies

If a company is "associated" with another company – that is, if they are both controlled by the same people, or one company controls the other, then the various bands are split between the associated companies.

For example, if Aunt Sally in Case Study 1 had decided to go ahead and invest in her niece's business, and they had set up a company of which she owned 60%, then because this company and Aunt Sally's other company would be "associated", each company would pay 20% tax on only the first £150,000 profit, and after that it would be paying at 32.5%

If three companies are associated, then the bands are divided between the three of them (only the first £100,000 at 20%), and so on.

3.3. Reducing the CT Bands

The rate bands are also reduced if a company prepares its accounts for a period of less than a year – so if the accounts are for 10 months, the small companies' rate band will be £250,000 (300,000 x 10/12).

3.4. Key Dates for the Company

A company must decide on the date to which it will prepare its accounts – its **accounting reference date.**

A company normally has the same accounting reference date every year, so that its **period of account** is the year ending on the accounting reference date.

If a company wishes, it can change its accounting reference date, so that the period of account in which the date is changed is longer or shorter than one year – but it cannot be longer than 18 months.

For the purposes of corporation tax, companies are taxed on the profits they make in their **accounting period.**

This is normally the same as the company's period of account, so that if a company's accounting date is 31 December (the most popular date) then its period of account will be the year ending on 31 December, and its accounting period for corporation tax purposes will also be the year ending 31 December.

In some circumstances, there may be a difference between the company's period of account and its accounting period. This is because the tax legislation includes rules for when a company's accounting period ends, and these mean that an accounting period for tax purposes may end on a different day to the company's accounting date.

For corporation tax purposes, a company's accounting period comes to an end at the earliest of the following dates:

- 12 months after it started (whereas a company's accounts may cover up to 18 months)
- The date the company chooses as its accounting date (so for example, if the accounting period begins on 1 January, and the company decides to change its accounting date to 31 October, it will have a 10 month accounting period for that year)
- The date the company becomes liable to corporation tax (such as when it gets a source of income)
- The date the company begins trading

- The date the company stops trading

- The date the **winding up** of the company begins (that is, when the process of ending the company's existence starts)

In cases where the company's accounting period (for tax) is not the same as its period of account, the tax inspector will apportion the profits of the period of account to arrive at the profits of the accounting period – this most often happens when the company's period of account is longer than one year.

The apportionment is normally done on a time basis, but the inspector (or the company) can look at the dates of specific transactions if this gives a fairer result – for example, if a large part of the company's profit for the period of account came from one transaction such as the sale of a property, this could be put into the accounting period when it occurred rather than apportioned over more than one period.

3.5. Benefiting from the Favourable Company Taxes

Rates of tax for companies may seem very favourable, compared to income tax at 22% (or 40% for taxable income over £34,600).

Case Study - 2 Favourable Company Taxes

Bill has a property portfolio of 10 buy to let properties.

After all expenses, the rentals from these properties produce a profit of £20,000 per year. Because the portfolio is held within a company, the company must pay CT of £4,000 (£20,000 at 20%).

If Bill owned the properties directly, the income tax he would pay would depend on how much other income he had for the year, but it would probably be between £4,400 (£20,000 at 22%) and £8,000 (£20,000 at 40%).

Golden Rule

The above case study, however, misses out the most important point about companies as compared to sole traders or partnerships – once the company has paid its CT for the year, the remaining cash remains in the company, and there may be further tax costs in extracting it.

3.6. Extracting the Cash from the Company

There are essentially two ways of extracting cash from a company and both these methods are described in the following sections.

3.6.1. *Paying A Salary*

If the company pays a salary, it will have to operate PAYE on that salary, just like any other employer. It will also have to deduct National Insurance Contributions, and pay employers' National Insurance Contributions.

Case Study - 3 Extracting Money Using a Salary

If Bill has no other income for the year, and the company pays all its profits out to him as a salary, the tax works like this:

Company Profit (after deducting salary)	**NIL**
Employer's NIC on Salary	(1,679)
Salary net of employers NIC	18,320
Employee's NIC	(1,443)
Income tax	(2,613)
Cash in hand after PAYE	14,264
Effective rate of tax on £20,000	28.68%

If Bill had owned the properties directly, then his tax bill would have been:

Income from property	**20,000**
Deduct personal allowance	(5,225)
Taxable income	14,775
Income tax at 10%	(223)
Income tax at 22 %	(2,760)
Cash in hand after tax	17,017
Effective rate of tax on £20,000	14.92%

Note there is no National Insurance to pay, because letting property is not a trade. National insurance was payable on the salary from the company, however, as it is on all salaries.

3.6.2. *Paying Dividends*

The other way for Bill to extract the cash from his company is for the company to pay him a **dividend**.

A dividend is how a company distributes its profits to its shareholders. Unlike paying a salary, a company cannot deduct the dividends it pays from its profits chargeable to CT.

When shareholders receive a dividend, the rate of tax they pay depends on their other income for the tax year. If they are not liable to tax at the Higher Rate (taxable income over £34,600 for 2007/08), then the rate of income tax on their dividend is 10%.

A dividend, however, comes with a "tax credit" to reflect the CT the company has already paid on its profits, and so there will be no further income tax to pay:

Basic Rate Taxpayer	
Actual dividend paid	900
Add notional tax credit (1/9)	100
Taxable amount of dividend	1,000
Income tax on dividend at 10%	100
Deduct tax credit	(100)
Income tax payable	NIL

7.9 If the shareholder is liable to income tax at the Higher Rate, then the rate of tax on their dividend will be the "Dividend Income rate" of 32.5%, and they still get the tax credit, so it works like this:

Higher Rate Taxpayer	
Actual dividend paid	900
Add notional tax credit (1/9)	100
Taxable amount of dividend	1,000

Income tax on dividend at 32.5%	325
Deduct tax credit	(100)
Income tax payable	225

In practice, the effective rate of tax on a dividend for a higher rate taxpayer works out at 25% (£900 x 25% = £225), but it pays to remember how the tax is calculated:

Case Study - 4 Extracting Money Using a Dividend

Mr Mean hates paying higher rate tax. For 2007/08, he sees that the personal allowance is £5,225, and that the higher rate band does not begin until £34,600 of taxable income.

He therefore arranges for his company to pay him a dividend of £39,825, thinking that he will have no income tax to pay because he will not be in the higher rate band. He has forgotten how the rates on dividends are calculated:

Mr Mean	
Actual dividend paid	39,825
Add notional tax credit (1/9)	4,425
Taxable amount of dividend	44,250
Deduct allowance and basic rate bands	(39,825)
Dividend taxable at 32.5%	4,425
Income tax on 4,425 at 32.5%	1,438
Deduct tax credit	(443)
Income tax payable	995

If Mr Mean really wanted to avoid paying higher rate tax, he should have paid himself a dividend of £35,843, because after adding the notional 1/9 tax credit, this comes to £39,825.

It seems clear, then, that dividends rather than salary are the way to extract cash from a company – but there can be cases where a mixture of the two provides the best solution.

3.6.3. Paying Dividends and A Salary

Case Study - 5 Extracting Money Using Both Dividend and a Salary (1)

Bill's property company makes a profit of £20,000 per year (see case study 3).

Bill has no other income for the year, so he pays himself a salary which is just below the "threshold" for income tax and NIC. The rest of the profit is paid out as a dividend:

	Company	**Cash for Bill**
Profit	20,000	
Deduct salary	(5,200)	5,200
Profit after salary	14,800	
Deduct CT on profit	(2,960)	
Profit after tax (dividend)	11,840	11,840
Total cash for Bill		17,040
Effective rate of tax	14.8%	

Bill has only saved £23 compared to the position if he had owned these properties directly (see Case Study 3), and this would in fact have been swallowed up by the additional costs of running a company.

On the whole, a company is unlikely to save enough money for a basic rate taxpayer to cover the additional cost of running a company.

Let us look at the position for a higher rate taxpayer:

Case Study - 6	Extracting Money Using Both Dividend and a Salary (2)

Ben has other income from investments which means he pays income tax at the 40% Higher Rate. He also has a property portfolio in a company which like Bill's yields £20,000 profit per year.

He uses the same strategy as Bill, paying himself a salary just below the "threshold":

	Company	Cash for Ben
Profit	20,000	
Deduct salary	(5,200)	5,200
Profit after salary	14,800	
Deduct CT on profit	(2,960)	
Profit after tax (dividend)	11,840	
Income tax on dividend	(2,960)	8,880
Total cash for Ben		14,080
Effective rate of tax	29.60%	

If Ben had owned the properties directly, he would have paid 40% tax on the £20,000 profit (£8,000), so he has saved £2,080.

Because he has used £5,200 of his personal allowance against his salary, however, he will pay £2,080 more tax on his investment income, so after allowing for the cost of running the company, he is actually worse off.

The position would be different if Ben had a salary from another source, so that he could not pay himself a salary below the "threshold" from his company.

If all the income had to come out as a dividend, the position would be:

	Company	Cash for Ben
Profit	20,000	
Deduct CT on profit	(4,000)	
Profit after tax (dividend)	16,000	
Income tax on dividend	(4,000)	
Total cash for Ben		12,000
Effective rate of tax	40%	

There is no tax saving, and after considering the cost of running the company, Ben is worse off than if he had held the properties in his own name.

So far, we have seen that there is little or no advantage in using a company compared to owning property directly, but in certain situations, it can still produce savings, as we shall see in the next chapter.

4. Building up a property portfolio using a company

In this chapter we will look at when it is beneficial to use a company to grow a property portfolio.

4.1. Using a Company to Grow Your Property Portfolio – a Detailed Case Study

A company comes into its own when the plan is to reinvest the rental profits in more property, rather than to draw them out for living expenses.

Jane has a well paid job, and pays income tax at 40%.

She wants to build up a portfolio of rented properties, using the profits from the rentals to fund the acquisition of other properties.

She begins with a portfolio of 10 buy to let properties, like Bill's, but instead of taking the profits out of the company, she leaves them there to fund the deposits on new properties.

Note that this example assumes that, as announced in the 2007 Budget, the rate of corporation tax for a small company will be 20% for Financial Year 2007, 21% for Financial Year 2008, and 22% for Financial Year 2009 and later years.

In the first year, the position will be:

	Company	**Direct ownership**
Profits	20,000	20,000
Cost of company	(1,000)	NIL
Profit after costs	19,000	20,000
Tax payable	(3,800)	(8,000)
Cash for reinvestment	15,200	12,000

If the pattern is repeated in the following year, the cash available for reinvestment in the company will be £30,210, compared to £24,000 if the properties are owned directly.

Let us assume that £20,000 is used to fund the deposit on a new property, and that as a result, the profit for the third year increases to £22,000:

Year 3	Company	Direct ownership
Profits	22,000	22,000
Cost of company	(1,000)	NIL
Profit after costs	21,000	22,000
Tax payable	(4,620)	(8,800)
Cash after tax	16,380	13,200
Add cash from previous years	30,210	24,000
Deduct deposit on new property	(20,000)	(20,000)
Cash for reinvestment	26,590	17,200

The company can afford to use another £20,000 to fund another deposit on another property, taking its profits to 24,000. If Jane owned the properties directly, she could not yet afford another deposit, so year 4 looks like this:

Year 4	Company	Direct ownership
Profits	24,000	22,000
Cost of company	(1,000)	NIL
Profit after costs	23,000	22,000
Tax payable	(5,060)	(8,800)
Cash after tax	17,940	13,200
Add cash from previous years	26,590	17,200
Deduct deposit on new property	(20,000)	N/A
Cash for reinvestment	24,530	30,400

The company can afford to spend another £20,000 on the deposit for yet another property, and this year, so could Jane as an individual:

Year 5	Company	Direct ownership
Profits	26,000	24,000
Cost of company	(1,000)	NIL
Profit after costs	25,000	24,000
Tax payable	(5,500)	(9,600)
Cash after tax	19,500	14,400
Add cash from previous years	24,530	30,400
Deduct deposit on new property	(20,000)	(20,000)
Cash for reinvestment	24,030	24,800

For year 6, both businesses can afford another deposit, so here is Year 6:

Year 6	Company	Direct ownership
Profits	28,000	26,000
Cost of company	(1,000)	NIL
Profit after costs	27,000	26,000
Tax payable	(5,940)	(10,400)
Cash after tax	21,060	15,600
Add cash from previous years	24,030	24,800
Deduct deposit on new property	(20,000)	(20,000)
Cash for reinvestment	25,090	20,400

For year 7, both businesses can again afford another deposit, so here is Year 7:

Year 7	Company	Direct ownership
Profits	30,000	28,000
Cost of company	(1,000)	NIL
Profit after costs	29,000	28,000
Tax payable	(6,380)	(11,200)
Cash after tax	22,620	16,800
Add cash from previous years	25,090	20,400
Deduct deposit on new property	(20,000)	(20,000)
Cash for reinvestment	27,710	17,200

For Year 8, only the company can afford a £20,000 deposit, so in Year 8:

Year 8	Company	Direct ownership
Profits	32,000	28,000
Cost of company	(1,000)	NIL
Profit after costs	31,000	28,000
Tax payable	(6,820)	(11,200)
Cash after tax	24,180	16,800
Add cash from previous years	27,710	17,200
Deduct deposit on new property	(20,000)	NIL
Cash for reinvestment	31,890	34,000

In Year 9, both buy another property:

Year 9	Company	Direct ownership
Profits	34,000	30,000
Cost of company	(1,000)	NIL
Profit after costs	33,000	30,000
Tax payable	(7,260)	(12,000)
Cash after tax	25,740	18,000
Add cash from previous years	31,890	34,000
Deduct deposit on new property	(20,000)	(20,000)
Cash for reinvestment	37,630	32,000

In year 10, both can buy one more property:

Year 10	Company	Direct ownership
Profits	36,000	32,000
Cost of company	(1,000)	NIL
Profit after costs	35,000	32,000
Tax payable	(7,700)	(12,800)
Cash after tax	27,300	19,200
Add cash from previous years	37,630	32,000
Deduct deposit on new property	(20,000)	(20,000)
Cash for reinvestment	44,930	31,200

If we summarise the results for the first ten years, we get:

	Company	Directly owned	Difference
Total income	**272,000**	**252,000**	**20,000**
Total running costs	**(10,000)**	**NIL**	**(10,000)**
Total tax paid	**(56,880)**	**(100,800)**	**43,920**
Total cash benefit			**53,920**
Number of properties in portfolio	**18**	**16**	**2**

So, by using a company, Jane would be £53,920 better off after ten years, and this is reflected in the fact that her property portfolio has grown by two more properties than it would have done had she owned the properties directly.

In the next chapter, we will look at another way to use a company to reduce tax on a property portfolio.

5. Using a Property Management Company

We have seen that a company can provide the best environment for growing a portfolio, if you do not want to take out the profits year by year for your own use.

In some cases, a Property Management Company can provide a useful half way house between private ownership and corporate ownership.

A property management company does not own property itself. It manages the properties owned by an individual, collecting the rents and dealing with repairs, etc., and charges a fee for doing so.

In this chapter we will understand the tax implications of using a property management company.

5.1. Starting the Property Management Company

Case Study - 7 Starting the Property Management Company

Gary pays income tax at 40%, and owns fifteen properties, which produce gross rents of £150,000 per year.

After expenses, including mortgage interest, the profit on these properties is £30,000 per year. Gary sets up a property management company, which charges him 12% of the gross rents for managing the properties:

	Gary	**Company**	**If no company**
Rents after expenses	**30,000**		**30,000**
Management fee	**(18,000)**	**18,000**	
Company admin		(1,000)	
Taxable profits	12,000	17,000	30,000
Tax	(4,800)	(3,400)	(12,000)
Cash after tax	7,200	13,600	
Dividend	13,600	(13,600)	
Tax on dividend	(3,400)		
Cash in hand	17,400		18,000

5.2. Growing the Property Management Company

Case Study - 8 Growing the Property Management Company

Because he extracted all the profits, Gary was worse off by £600, but if he had left the cash in the company, the position would have been:

	Gary	Company	If no company
Rents after expenses	30,000		30,000
Management fee	(18,000)	18,000	
Company admin		(1,000)	
Taxable profits	12,000	17,000	30,000
Tax	(4,800)	(3,400)	(12,000)
Cash after tax	7,200	13,600	18,000

The saving is now £2,800, but £13,600 of the cash is still in the company.

5.3. Getting the Cash Accumulated Out of Management Company

There are several possible ways Gary could deal with this:

- He could wind up the company.
  He would make a capital gain equivalent to the cash he got from the company, but there would be little or no capital gains tax to pay, assuming he had owned the shares for more than two years (we will look at capital gains tax later in this guide).

  Supposing he had run the company for three years, there would be 3 times £13,600 = £40,800 in the company, so the capital gain would be calculated like this:

Capital gain on shares	40,800
Deduct taper relief 75%	(30,600)
Chargeable	10,200

Deduct annual exemption	(9,200)
Taxable	1,000
CGT at 40%	(400)
Cash after tax	40,400
Effective rate of tax on £40,800	0.98%

Gary's total saving from this strategy is therefore 3 x £2,800 = £8,400, less CGT of £400, giving a saving over three years of £8,000.

Caution

There is anti-avoidance legislation which could be used by HMRC if this strategy is done too often, or too blatantly. Ideally, it needs to be combined with the sale of the properties, so that there is a commercial justification for winding up the management company.

- Gary could use the cash in the company to fund deposits on other properties to be purchased by the company, thus converting it into a property investment company.

  This can be a way of using such a company as a "stepping stone" to building up a property portfolio in a company, if you cannot afford to set one up from scratch.

- Gary could wait for a year in which his taxable income fell below the higher rate band (for example, when he retires), and then pay a dividend out of the company with no additional income tax to pay.

Property Management Companies are no longer the excellent tax saving vehicles they used to be, (when the rate of corporation tax on company profits under £10,000 was 0%), but they can still be a useful tool for accumulating cash at a lower rate of tax than that suffered by a direct investor in property.

6. Everything you need to Know About Dividend Payments

We have been talking about companies paying dividends, and it is important to understand the rules that apply to such payments.

In this chapter we will examine these rules more closely.

6.1. Working with "Distributable Profits"

A company can only pay a dividend out of its "distributable profits".

"Distributable profits" are a company's profits after paying its expenses and its corporation tax.

If it does not pay any dividends for a particular year, then those "distributable profits" will remain in the company's balance sheet, and can be used to pay a dividend next year:

Case Study - 9 Distributing the Profits

A new company is set up, and in its first two years, it makes a profit of £40,000 per year after all expenses. Its distributable profits are therefore:

Profit for year 1	40,000
CT due on profit	(8,000)
Distributable profits	32,000
Profit for year 2	40,000
CT due on profit	(8,400)
Distributable profits	63,600

In the third year, the company has a bad year, and makes a loss of £10,000 after all expenses. Its distributable profits are now:

Distributable profits at start of year	63,600
Deduct loss for year	(10,000)

Distributable profits at end of year	55,700

Things go better in the fourth year, with a profit of £15,000, and the company decides to pay a dividend of £10,000:

Distributable profits at start of year	55,700
Add profit for year	15,000
Deduct CT due on profit	(3,300)
Distributable profits	67,400
Dividend paid	(10,000)
Distributable profits at end of year	57,400

6.2. Who Gets the Dividends?

Dividends are paid to the company's shareholders according to how many shares they own – so in a simple case where all the shares are of the same "class", each shareholder gets a dividend proportional to his shareholding.

Case Study - 10 Proportioning the Dividends

The shares in a company are owned as follows:

Mary Jones (wife)	40 £1 Ordinary Shares
Joe Jones (husband)	40 £1 Ordinary Shares
Sue Jones (adult daughter)	20 £1 Ordinary Shares
Total	100 £1 Ordinary Shares

If the company pays a dividend of £10,000, that is equivalent to £100 per share, so the three shareholders will each receive:

Mary	£4,000
Joe	£4,000
Sue	£2,000
Total	£10,000

6.3. The Two Types of Dividend

It is important that the formalities are properly observed when a company pays dividends. There are two basic types of dividend:

6.3.1. A "Final" Dividend.

This is a dividend paid out of the company's distributable profits after its accounting period ends.

The Annual General Meeting (AGM) of the shareholders approves the company's accounts for the year, and also approves the payment of a "final" dividend, which is then said to have been "declared".

Although the final dividend may not in fact be paid until some time later, it is treated as payable for income tax purposes on the day it is "declared" (typically, the date of the AGM), unless exceptionally the declaration specifies a different date for the payment.

6.3.2. An "Interim" Dividend.

This is a dividend paid by a company during the year. It is approved by the directors of the company, who must be satisfied there are enough "distributable reserves" to pay the dividend. For income tax purposes, an interim dividend is treated as paid on the date it is actually paid.

Golden Rule

It is <u>essential</u> that the directors are satisfied there are sufficient distributable profits before they approve the payment of an interim dividend, and this means having accurate and up to date records of the company's income and expenses.

We shall see below what can happen if the directors pay a dividend without taking this precaution.

6.4. Getting the Paperwork Right

It is also essential to produce the correct paperwork for a dividend. This means having:

- A minute of the meeting at which it was decided to pay the dividend
- A "dividend voucher" for each shareholder

6.4.1. Sample – Meeting Minute

Here is a sample wording for the minute of a resolution to pay an interim dividend:

Property Company Limited
Company Registration No. 12345678

1, Any Road
Anywhere
PO1 1PO

Minutes of a Meeting of the Board of Directors

Date of the meeting held at the Registered Office of the Company: **02/04/07**

Present:

Mr Joseph Jones (Director)
Mrs Susan Jones (Director and Company Secretary)

DIVIDENDS

It was resolved that the company pay an interim dividend in respect of the period ending **31/12/07** to holders registered as at **02/04/07** as follows:

Share class	Dividend rate	Date to be paid
Ordinary of £1	**£100 per share**	**02/04/07**

ANY OTHER BUSINESS:

There being no further business the meeting was closed.

J Jones
……………………………………………..
Signed on Behalf of the Board

Name: J Jones Date: 02/04/07 Position: Director

Notice that the amount of the dividend is expressed as so much *per share.*

6.4.2. *Sample – Dividend Voucher*

Here is an example of a dividend voucher. One of these must be given to each shareholder when the dividend is paid:

Property Company Limited

Company Registration No. 12345678

1, Any Road
Anytown
PO1 1PO

Tax Voucher

Interim dividend for the period ending 31st December 2007 to shareholders registered on 2nd April 2007

Payment Date
02/04/07

Shareholder Details
Mrs Mary Jones 1, Any Road Anytown PO1 1PO

Shareholding	Dividend rate	Dividend Payment	Tax Credit
40 Ordinary shares of £1	**£100 per share**	**£4,000**	**£444.44p**

This voucher should be kept. It will be accepted by HM Revenue & Customs as evidence of a tax credit.

Susan Jones
……………………………………………
(company secretary)

Date:

10.11 It may seem a nuisance putting this paperwork in place, but I have seen too many companies get themselves into trouble by not doing this properly.

6.5. Two Pitfalls to Avoid when Making Dividend Payments

Two of the commonest problems with company dividends are:

6.5.1. Illegal Dividends.

If the company pays a dividend that cannot be covered by its distributable profits, the shareholders will have to repay the dividend to the company, and they and the company may be taxed on the basis that instead of paying them a dividend, the company made a loan to them.

The company would have to pay tax at 25% on the amount of the dividend, which would only be repaid to the company once the shareholders had repaid the dividend.

6.5.2. Timing of Dividends

Too often, a company's shareholders simply draw the cash they need from the company, and then declare a dividend at the end of the year equivalent to the cash they have taken from the company.

If this practice is discovered by HMRC, such as during an investigation of the company, the onus will be on the shareholders to prove that the cash they took out during the year was a loan from the company, which was repaid by the dividends declared after the end of the year, and not a disguised salary (on which, of course, PAYE and NIC will be due).

6.6. Using Dividend Waivers – An Effective Tax Planning Tool

It is possible for a shareholder to waive his right to a dividend.

This might be done because he had enough income for the year, and did not want to pay tax on the dividend when he did not need the money.

Provided the following issues are carefully considered, a dividend waiver can be an effective tax planning tool.

Caution

Take care – dividend waivers are likely to be closely looked at by HMRC to see if they have been done properly, and there may be extra tax to pay if they are not.

A dividend cannot be waived once it has become payable, so interim dividends must be waived before they are paid, but final dividends must be waived before they are declared.

The waiver will take the form of a written document in which the shareholder gives up his right to the dividend. It is best to have this drafted by a solicitor, in the form of a Deed.

The minutes of the meeting at which the dividend is paid (interim) or declared (final) should include a reference to the fact that the Company Secretary produced a waiver of the dividend due to Mr X, and make it clear this was done before the dividend was declared or paid.

6.7. Watch out for the "Settlements" Legislation

It is essential that the waiver cannot be attacked under the "settlements" legislation. It is easiest to explain this with an example.

Case Study - 11 "Settlements" Legislation

Before the meeting at which the dividend in Case Study - 10 is paid, Joe (who pays tax at 40%) decides he does not want a dividend from the company, because he and Mary (who only pays tax at the basic rate) have enough other income for the year and Joe would prefer not to pay income tax on a dividend he does not need. He has a Dividend Waiver drafted by his solicitor and "executes" it (this is lawyer-speak for signing it in front of a witness) then gives it to his daughter Sue, the company secretary.

The interim dividend of £100 per share is therefore paid to Mary and Sue, but not to Joe:

	Company	Mary	Joe	Sue
Distributable profits	10,000			
Dividends Paid	(6,000)	4,000	Waived	2,000
Distributable profits	4,000			

This should be acceptable to HMRC, but supposing the company decided to pay a dividend of £150 per share:

	Company	Mary	Joe	Sue
Distributable profits	10,000			
Dividends Paid	(9,000)	6,000	Waived	3,000
Distributable profits	1,000			

HMRC will argue that of that £9,000 dividend, £3,000 should be taxed on Joe!

This may seem illogical at first, but consider what would have happened if Joe had not waived his right to a dividend, and a payment of £150 per share had been made:

	Company	**Mary**	**Joe**	**Sue**
Distributable profits	**10,000**			
Dividends Paid	**(15,000)**	6,000	6,000	3,000
Distributable profits	**Minus 5,000, so Illegal dividend**			

In other words, the only reason why the company was able to pay Mary £6,000 and Sue £3,000, instead of £4,000 and £2,000 respectively, **was because Joe had waived his right to his dividends.**

HMRC will say that Joe has made a "settlement" of £3,000 of his income on Sue and Mary. This is a highly technical area of the law, and there are arguments against HMRC's point of view, but what is certain is that using a waiver in this way is likely to lead to time-consuming and expensive enquiries from HMRC.

7. The Property Development Company

So far in this guide, we have been considering the position of a property investor – someone who buys property in order to enjoy the rents from it.

In this chapter will now consider the property developer.

7.1. The Property Developer

A **property developer** buys property (or sometimes bare land) with the intention of improving the property (or building a new property) and selling it on in the short term, at a profit.

Golden Rule

The important distinction for tax purposes is that a property developer is **trading**.

He will pay income tax on the profits he makes from selling the properties, whereas the property investor will pay capital gains tax if and when he sells one of his investment properties.

An individual who is trading in property will also be liable to pay National Insurance Contributions (NIC) on his profits, unless he is over the state pension age (currently 65 for men and 60 for women).

7.2. Companies and Property Developers

This gives us a rather different picture when we compare trading as an individual property developer with doing the same thing through a company.

Case Study - 12 Using a Company For Your Property Development Activities

Dave trades as a property developer through a limited company. He has other income from his investments, so he pays income tax at 40%. His company makes a profit of £100,000 for the year. If he draws out all the profits from the company as dividends, plus a salary just below the "threshold" (see Case Study 5), his tax position will be:

	Company	Cash for Dave	If no company	Saving
Profit	100,000		100,000	

Company running costs	(1,000)			
Profit	93,800			
CT due	(18,760)			
Distributable profit (dividend)	75,040	75,040		
Income tax		(18,760)	(40,000)	
NIC			(3,135)	
Cash for Dave		61,480	56,865	4,615

Of course, as in Case Study 6, he will pay an extra £2,080 tax on his investment income because he has used £5,200 of his personal allowance against his salary, so his real saving is only £2,535

If Dave had a high salary from another job, so that he could not take advantage of the "below the threshold" salary from his company, the position would be:

	Company	**Cash for Dave**	**If no company**	**Saving**
Profit	100,000		100,000	
Company running costs	(1,000)			
Profit	99,000			
CT due	(19,800)			
Distributable profit (dividend)	79,200	79,200		
Income tax		(19,800)	(40,000)	
NIC			(1,114)*	
Cash for Dave		59,400	58,886	514

* Because Dave has a substantial salary from another job, his Class 4 self-employed contributions will be refunded to him, except for those at the 1% rate.

Once again, it is clear that there is little advantage in using a company if you are going to want to extract all the profits for your personal use.

If your strategy is to leave the profits in the company and use them to finance further development, however, having a property development company will offer the same tax benefits as it does to a property investor – see section 4.1.

If you are already trading as a property developer, as a sole trader or a partnership, and you feel it would be beneficial to transfer the business into a company so as to take advantage of the lower rates of tax on your profits (provided you leave them in the company), there is an important relief from tax you can take advantage of – incorporation relief. This is dealt with later in this guide.

7.3. The Construction Industry Scheme ("CIS")

An important note on the Construction Industry Scheme ("CIS")

The CIS requires property developers to deduct tax from certain payments to tradesmen, and in other cases to record amounts paid and make regular returns to HMRC of those amounts. The details of this scheme are beyond the scope of this guide, but a number of smaller property development businesses are not aware that they come within this scheme, and as a result may face penalties for failure to operate the scheme. There is no minimum level below which the scheme does not apply to a property developer.

The CIS does not apply to buy to let investors, (unless they spend over £1million on construction work each year!), but it applies to ALL property developers.

Full details of the CIS can be found in **"Tax Secrets for Property Developers and Renovators"**.

I am the author of this guide, and it is available through www.property-tax-portal.co.uk.

8. Incorporation Relief

In this chapter we will look at a relief that is available when assets are transferred into a company which you control.

This relief is known as Incorporation Relief.

8.1. Transferring Assets into Your Company

If you transfer any asset you own to a company which you control, for tax purposes you will be treated as having disposed of it at its market value, so you may well find yourself making a capital gain and paying CGT.

There are, however, two forms of tax relief that may help to solve this problem and these are detailed in the following sections.

8.1.1. Holdover Relief for Gifts of Business Assets

This applies when a person carrying on a trade makes a gift of an asset used for that trade, or sells it at less than its market value.

A claim can be made to "hold over" the gain on the difference between the **market value** of the asset gifted or sold at less than market value, and the **amount (if any) actually paid for it.**

Case Study - 13 Holdover Relief

Rita owns five cottages, which she bought seven years ago with a legacy from her grandmother, and which she lets out to tourists as "furnished holiday accommodation". This is treated as a trade for tax purposes (see **"Tax Secrets for Property Developers and Renovators"** for details of how a property can qualify as "furnished holiday accommodation").

The cottages each produce a rental profit of £10,000 per year.

Rita does not intend to sell these cottages – she regards them as her "pension fund" and would like to be able to leave them to her children when she dies.

Because at the moment she has a highly paid job, and does not need all the income from these cottages, her Tax Adviser suggests that she might benefit from transferring these cottages into a company.

She bought each cottage seven years ago for £50,000, and they are now worth £150,000 each, so she would make a capital gain of £100,000 on each cottage.

Because she is entitled to "business asset taper relief" on the cottages, any gain she made would be reduced by 75%, so the gain she would pay CGT on would be £25,000 for each cottage.

Her Tax Adviser suggests she sets up a company, and sells the cottages to it for £57,360 each, and makes a claim to "hold-over" the rest of the gain.

This seems an odd sum, but he explains that the tax calculation will work like this:

"Sale" proceeds of 5 cottages	**286,800**
Less cost of cottages	**(250,000)**
Capital gain	**36,800**
Taper relief (75%)	**(27,600)**
Chargeable gain	**9,200**
Annual CGT exempt amount for 2007/08	**(9,200)**
Taxable gains for year	**NIL**

The company does not pay Rita £286,800 in cash. Instead it credits her with having lent this money to the company. Rita will be able to draw this loan out of the company as and when she needs the money, and without paying any income tax.

Meanwhile, the company is only paying 20% tax on the rents it receives, instead of the 40% income tax Rita was paying. On the combined rental profits of £50,000, this is a tax saving of £10,000 per year – reducing to £8,000 per year after 2009, when the corporation tax rate will be 22%.

There is one downside to this, however. For the purposes of Stamp Duty Land Tax, the properties are treated as transferred to the company at their market value, and so the company will have to pay SDLT on £750,000, which will cost it £30,000.

Rita must decide if this cost (equivalent to just under three years' worth of the tax saving she will make) is worth paying.

Note that this strategy is specific to Rita's circumstances, and in particular to the fact that she intends to leave the holiday cottages to her children.

If she intended to sell them herself, she would probably do better to keep them in her personal ownership, because of the availability to her of business taper relief (which is not available to a company – see Chapter 9), and the fact that the "cost" of the cottages in the company will be £57,360 per cottage (the amount that the company paid her for them).

8.1.2. Incorporation in Exchange for Shares

12.4 There is another type of incorporation relief, which applies when a business is transferred to a company and instead of paying cash, the company issues shares in exchange for the assets.

It works like this:

Case Study - 14 Incorporation in Exchange for Shares

Bill has a business with a market value of £100,000. If he were to sell it for that sum, he would make a capital gain of £70,000. He sets up a company, and transfers the business to the company. The company does not pay him anything for the business. Instead, it issues 1,000 £1 Ordinary shares to him.

From the company's point of view, it now owns a business worth £100,000, and the "cost" of that business from the company's point of view is £100,000 – so if it sold the business tomorrow, it would not make a capital gain.

From Bill's point of view, he now owns 1,000 shares worth £100 each (value of company = £100,000, divided by the 1,000 shares).

Because he qualifies for "Incorporation relief" on this transaction, he is not charged any capital gains tax, but the gain he would have been taxed on is deducted from the "cost" of his shares for CGT purposes, so the cost of his shares is deemed to be £30 each (£100,000 - £70,000 = £30,000, divided by the 1,000 shares).

The fact that the company is treated as acquiring the business at its market value offers another planning opportunity:

Case Study - 15 Incorporation Followed by Sale of Business

John has a business with a market value of £2,000,000. He wants to sell it, and use the sale proceeds to buy a portfolio of investment properties, which he sees as his "retirement fund".

If he simply sold the business, he would make a capital gain of £1,600,000, which would be "tapered" to £400,000, on which CGT of £160,000 would be due.

Instead, he transfers the business to a company in exchange for shares. The company issues 1,000 shares to him in exchange for the business. The position is therefore:

The company now owns the business, which for capital gains purposes "cost" it £2,000,000. John has 1,000 shares worth £2,000,000, but which for CGT purposes "cost" him £400,000 (after deducting the capital gain of £1,600,000).

The company now sells the business for £2,000,000. Because its cost to the company was £2,000,000, the company makes no gain at all and has no tax to pay. The company can spend the whole £2,000,000 on investment properties, and John will have a more comfortable retirement than if he had sold the business himself.

8.2. Watch Out for Three Pitfalls

The previous case study looks almost too good to be true, and like most such things, there are a number of pitfalls that one needs to be wary of.

These pitfalls are detailed as follows.

8.2.1. "Preordained Series of Transactions"

There is a rule of law developed by the courts which allows HMRC to disregard a transaction if it is part of a series of transactions which were set up in advance, and the transaction in question was "inserted" simply for the purpose of avoiding tax.

In other words, HMRC would say that the reality was that John sold the business himself, and the transfer to the company was "inserted" purely for tax avoidance. For this reason, it would be most important that John had not started the process of selling the business before he transferred it to the company.

Anyone contemplating using the same strategy as John should take advice from a Tax Adviser on whether HMRC would be likely to attack it as "preordained".

8.2.2. Stamp Duty Land Tax

As we have already seen, SDLT is charged on the market value of a property when it is transferred to a company, so if a substantial part of the value of John's business was in the property it owned, there would be a SDLT cost to factor into the equation.

8.2.3. What is a "Business"?

The legislation uses the word "business", but HMRC interpret the meaning of this word quite narrowly. In particular, they take the view that a property investment business is not normally a "business" for the purposes of incorporation relief.

I have heard of cases where property investment businesses have been transferred to companies and managed to get incorporation relief.

Where the business involves a great deal of management and is very "hands on" for the proprietor, it is possible that HMRC would not dispute the relief, but each case needs to be looked at on its merits, and there can be no guarantees that there will not be a challenge from HMRC.

In some cases, however, it may be worthwhile taking the risk.

8.3. Incorporating an Existing Property Investment Portfolio

Case Study - 16 Incorporating an Investment Portfolio

Jill has a business of exactly the same value as John's in Case Study - 15, except that it consists of several investment properties. She wants to sell these, and invest the money in buying a hotel.

She has been to a leading Tax Counsel, who has advised her that there is a good chance that her business would qualify for incorporation relief. He stresses that there is still a risk that it would be challenged by HMRC, however.

If Jill simply sells her properties, she will make a gain of £1,600,000, just like John. Her investment properties do not qualify for business taper relief, however, so her CGT bill could be as high as £640,000. If she transfers the business to a company AND her incorporation relief is not denied by HMRC, the only cost will be the SDLT of £80,000 on the transfer of the properties to the company.

If the incorporation relief is denied, she will pay CGT of £640,000, but the company will still make no capital gain. It will, however, have paid the £80,000 SDLT.

Jill must decide if the possible saving of £560,000 (CGT £640,000 less SDLT of £80,000) is worth the risk of the extra cost of £80,000 SDLT.

8.4. Incorporating an Existing Property Development Business

A property development business is a trading activity, and so it would qualify for either of the incorporation reliefs referred to in this chapter.

It is therefore possible to transfer an existing property development (partnership or sole trader) into a company, with the only cost being the SDLT involved.

It must be remembered that the land owned by a property development business is its **trading stock** and not an asset liable to CGT, so that the uplift in the market value described in Case Study - 14 and Case Study - 15 will not apply to the land.

There will still be the advantage, however, of the company's profits being taxed at lower rates than the profits for an individual.

A refinement of this technique can be used where land that was originally acquired as an investment is going to be developed.

Case Study - 17 Incorporating a Property Development Business

Sylvia inherits some land from her grandmother.

The land is on the outskirts of a town, and Sylvia just uses it to graze her horse for four years. She then learns that it should now be possible to get planning permission to build three houses on the land. Sylvia would like to develop the land herself, and use the profits to start up a property development business.

Having read Chapter 4 in this guide, she knows it will be possible to grow the business much faster if she uses a property development company, but she has a problem.

The land, which was valued at £20,000 when she inherited it from her grandmother, is now worth £250,000, because of the prospect of getting planning permission. If she transfers the land to a company, the CGT she will pay will be:

Market value of land	250,000
Less value at grandmother's death	(20,000)
Gain	230,000
Taper relief (non-business) 10%	(23,000)
Chargeable gain	207,000
Annual exemption	(9,200)
Taxable	197,800
CGT at 40%	79,120

Sylvia's Tax Adviser has a suggestion, however. He tells Sylvia to set herself up as a property developer, by informing HMRC that she has decided to start trading, registering for the CIS (see section 7.3), and beginning the process of obtaining detailed planning permission, organising contracts to do the groundwork, and so on.

By doing this, Sylvia will have "appropriated" the land to her trading stock as a property developer.

This counts as a disposal for CGT, but he tells her to make an election under section 161 (3) of the Taxation of Chargeable Gains Act 1992.

The effect of this is that her property development business is treated as acquiring the land at its original value of £20,000, and Sylvia does not have any CGT to pay.

After having traded in her own name for long enough (and how long will depend on the circumstances, but is unlikely to be as much as a year) to make it clear that she is genuinely trading as a property developer, Sylvia can now transfer her business to a company.

Because the land is now trading stock, it can be transferred to the company at its book value, so Sylvia does not make a profit in her own name, and when the houses are completed and sold, the profit will be taxed at corporation tax rates, instead of at 40% in her hands. Note that the company will have to pay SDLT of £2,500, based on the market value of the land.

This same technique could be used by a buy to let investor who decided that one of his properties had development potential – he could "appropriate it to trading stock" and then transfer it to a property development company, just as Sylvia did with her grazing land.

9. Taper relief for CGT

In this chapter we will look at an important tax relief that was introduced in 1998 – Taper Relief.

This relief applies only to individuals (and trustees and executors). It does NOT apply to companies.

Taper relief reduces the amount of a capital gain that is charged to CGT, depending on how long the asset has been owned.

9.1. Taper Relief for Business Assets

For **business assets,** the rate of taper is as follows:

Number of complete years asset owned	Percentage of gain charged to CGT
Less than one year	100%
One year	50%
Two years or more	25%

So, for example, if you make a gain of £100,000 on a business asset you have owned for three years, you will pay CGT on £25,000 (ignoring your annual exemption for the purpose of this example). At 40%, this would be £10,000 – an effective rate of 10% tax on the gain.

9.2. Taper Relief for Non Business Assets

For any other assets ("Non-business assets"), the rate is:

Number of complete years asset owned since April 1998	Percentage of gain charged to CGT
Less than three years	100%
Three years	95%
Four years	90%

Five years	85%
Six years	80%
Seven years	75%
Eight years	70%
Nine years	65%
Ten years or more	60%

So for non-business assets, even after ten years of ownership, on a gain of £100,000 you would be taxed on £60,000. At 40%, this would be £24,000 – an effective rate of 24% on the gain. Just to make things more confusing, in the case of an asset owned since before 17 March 1998, and sold before 5 April 2008, there is a "bonus year" added to your period of ownership. After April 1998, you will have owned the asset for 10 years anyway, so the bonus year will no longer be relevant.

9.3. What is a "Business Asset?"

A "**business asset"** for taper relief purposes is:

1. An asset used for the purposes of a trade by:
   - An individual
   - A partnership
   - A "qualifying company" (more on this in a moment)

2. Shares in a "qualifying company"

9.4. What is a "Qualifying Company?"

The definition of a **"qualifying company"** is complicated, and to make things worse has changed several times since taper relief was introduced. Rather than go into the intricate details, there are two key points for property businesses:

- An unlisted company that does nothing but trade WILL be a qualifying company, so a pure property development company will be a qualifying company

- A company whose business is more than 20% non trading WILL NOT be a qualifying company – so a property investment company will not be a qualifying company

There are a number of points to consider about taper relief and property businesses. These are detailed in the following sections.

9.5. Business Taper Relief and Commercial Properties

An individual who is the landlord of a commercial property will be entitled to Business Taper Relief if his property is occupied by:

- An individual or a partnership that uses the premises to carry on a trade
- A qualifying company that carries on a trade

Case Study - 18 Business Taper Relief and Commercial Properties (1)

Ranjan owns a building that consists of a shop with rooms above it.

His tenants are a married couple who run a printing business in the shop, and use the rooms upstairs for office space and storage of paper and other materials for the business.

After Ranjan has owned this property for two years, he could sell it and only 25% of the gain he made would be charged to CGT.

Case Study - 19 Business Taper Relief and Commercial Properties (2)

Same facts as Case Study - 18, except that the married couple live in the upstairs flat as their home, instead of using it for business purposes.

If Ranjan sold this property, the gain would have to be apportioned between the downstairs and the upstairs, because only the downstairs would qualify for business asset taper relief.

Broadly speaking, if he sold the property after owning it for five years, half the gain would qualify for business taper relief, and half would only qualify for non-business taper relief:

	Business Asset (Shop)	Non business asset (Flat above)	Totals
Gain on sale	100,000	100,000	200,000
Business taper (75%)	(75,000)	NIL	(75,000)
Non business taper (15%)	NIL	(15,000)	(15,000)
Chargeable gain	25,000	85,000	110,000
Tax at 40%	10,000	34,000	44,000
Effective rate of tax on gain	10%	34%	22%

In practice, Ranjan might be able to argue that more of the gain should be apportioned to the shop (because it is more valuable than the flat above), but nevertheless, a significant part of the gain would miss out on business taper relief.

9.6. Business Taper Relief on Shares

Because a property development company is a trading company, its shares qualify for business taper relief.

If, however, it has any properties it lets out, there is a risk that it will fail to qualify.

Case Study - 20 Business Taper Relief on Shares

Rowley sets up a company for the purpose of buying some land, developing it by building three houses, and selling them.

The whole process takes just over two years. If he had done this himself as an individual, the position would be:

Profit on sale of houses	250,000
Income tax at 40%	(100,000)
NIC	(4635)
Cash for Rowley	145,365

Because he uses a company, the tax on the development profit is:

Profit on sale of houses	250,000
Cost of running company	(2,000)
Two years "threshold" salary for Rowley	(10,400)
Taxable profit	237,600
Corporation tax at 20% then 21% in year 2	(48,708)
Cash in Company	188,892

If Rowley then liquidates the company, he gets the following result:

Cash from company	188,892
CGT on gain on shares	(18,889)
Cash for Rowley	170,003
Add threshold salary	10,400
Total cash	180,403
Cash if done as sole trader	(145,365)
Saving produced by company	35,038

Note that this saving is only possible because the development has taken two years, thus allowing business asset taper relief to reach its maximum on the shares. The "threshold" salary will also have increased his income tax on his investments by £4,160, so the real saving is £33,013.

There is also anti-avoidance legislation that HMRC could invoke, if Rowley were to make a habit of doing this. Where the development is a "one-off" venture and he does not then do the same thing again, he has a better chance of not being attacked by the anti-avoidance legislation, but this is still a riskier strategy than most in this guide.

Finally, it should be remembered that there may be practical difficulties in liquidating the company, particularly as it has built and sold residential property – in some cases, there can be continuing liabilities for the developer after the sale. These are beyond the scope of this guide, but they need to be considered.

Most of the problems with taper relief occur because of the ease with which a company's shares can cease to qualify for business asset taper.

For example, if Rowley in Case Study - 20 had delayed liquidating his company after the last property was sold, some of his gain on the shares (relating to the period between the end of the company's trade and the date it was liquidated) would not qualify for business taper, and there would have to be an apportionment of the gain similar to the one in Case Study - 19.

10. Reinvestment Relief

In this chapter we will look at "Reinvestment Relief". Numerous questions are asked about this relief and we will try to get to grips with the most common scenarios when this relief may be considered.

10.1. Property Investors and Reinvestment Relief

Property investors often ask if they can defer paying CGT on gains they have made by reinvesting the money in another property.

Unfortunately, this is generally not possible.

There are only two exceptions:

10.1.1. Business Assets

A company (or an individual or partnership) which is carrying on a trade can claim "rollover relief" from tax on its capital gains if it sells an asset it has used for its trade and spends all the sale proceeds on buying another asset to use in its trade.

The new asset must be purchased within the period that begins one year before the old asset is sold, and ends three years after that sale.

There are several categories of asset that qualify for this relief, and among them are land and buildings which are occupied and used for the purposes of the trade being carried on.

This type of rollover relief is unlikely to be of much use to the property business, It will not apply to the buy to let investor, because he is not carrying on a trade, and it will not apply to the buildings sold by a property developer, because these buildings are his trading stock and he makes a profit chargeable to income tax when he sells them, not a capital gain.

10.1.2. Furnished Holiday Lettings

These are a special category of buy to let property – see Case Study - 13 – and rollover relief is available if one of these properties is sold and the proceeds used to buy another property.

Case Study - 21	**Furnished Holiday Lettings and Reinvestment Relief**

Chris owns a cottage which he lets according to the rules for "furnished holiday accommodation" (see **"Tax Secrets for Property Developers & Renovators"** for details of these rules). The cottage cost him £50,000 six years ago, and he sells it for £200,000.

The gain of £150,000 will be "tapered" by 75% because this type of letting is deemed to be a trade for some tax purposes, so he has a taxable gain of £37,500, on which he would pay £15,000 at the 40% tax rate.

Chris spends £220,000 on another holiday cottage one year after the sale of the old one. He has used the entire amount of the sale proceeds from the old cottage to buy the new one, so all of the capital gain on the old cottage is "rolled over" into the new one. When Chris comes to sell the new cottage, its cost for the purposes of CGT will be reduced by the amount of the gain that has been rolled over into it:

Amount spent on new cottage	220,000
Deduct capital gain rolled over from old cottage	(150,000)
Cost of new cottage for CGT purposes	70,000

Note that the gain rolled over is the gain before taper relief.

There is some relief even if you do not reinvest all the sale proceeds. Suppose that the new cottage cost Chris only £180,000. This is less than the sale proceeds of the old cottage, so the computation goes like this:

First, find the amount of the sale proceeds not reinvested. Here, this is £20,000 (£200,000 - £180,000). This is less than the capital gain of £150,000 on the old cottage, so the amount of the gain that has not been reinvested is £20,000.

Chris will be taxed on a gain of £20,000, and the cost for CGT purposes of the new cottage will be:

Amount spent on new cottage	180,000
Deduct capital gain rolled over from old cottage	(130,000)
Cost of new cottage for CGT purposes	50,000

There is one other point to bear in mind about furnished holiday accommodation.

Because it would be possible for a person to roll a gain on an old holiday cottage over into a new one, and then move into it as his main residence and so exempt it from CGT, the relief is only given provisionally, and if when the new property is sold it qualifies for relief from CGT as a main residence, the gain previously held over is brought back into charge.

There is one other way to defer a capital gain by reinvesting the proceeds of a sale. This is by using the **Enterprise Investment Scheme ("EIS")** for individuals, and the **"Corporate Venturing Scheme" ("CVS") for companies**. These are schemes that both offer tax advantages for investment in the appropriate sort of company.

The schemes are not identical, but they share many features.

10.2. Deferring Capital Gains by Reinvesting

10.2.1. Enterprise Investment Scheme (EIS)

The **EIS** offers three forms of tax relief to an individual who invests in new shares in an EIS company:

- Income tax relief (at 20%) on the amount (up to £400,000) invested in EIS shares, provided that the individual is not "connected" with the company – that is, he and his "associates" do not own more than 30% of it.

- If the shares qualify for the above income tax relief, and they are later sold at a loss, that loss can be deducted from the investor's income for the year.

- If the shares qualify for the income tax relief, and are sold at a profit after more than three years, the profit is exempt from CGT, except for any gains "deferred" – see next bullet point.

- Deferral of capital gains on **any amount** reinvested in EIS shares – this relief applies whether or not the individual is "connected" to the EIS company, and is the one we shall concentrate on here.

  The investment must be made within the same time limit as for rollover relief – one year before to three years after the gain to be deferred.

An EIS company must meet certain conditions if it is to be a "qualifying company" and its shareholders can get tax relief on their investment.

The detailed rules are very complicated, and expert tax advice is essential if you are contemplating an EIS investment, but in outline:

- The company must not be listed on a Stock Market

- It must not be controlled by another company

- It must carry on a "qualifying trade" wholly or mainly in the UK

A qualifying trade is defined by excluding certain types of trade – any other trade will be a "qualifying trade".

The following are **"excluded activities"** and a company which carries on any of these trades will **not** be a "qualifying company" for EIS purposes:

- Dealing in land, commodities, shares or other financial instruments
- Dealing in goods (except for ordinary wholesalers and retailers)
- Banking, insurance, money-lending, and other financial activities
- Leasing or receiving royalties or licence fees
- Providing legal or accountancy services
- Property development
- Farming or market gardening
- Woodlands or forestry activities
- Running hotels or similar establishments
- Running nursing homes or residential care homes

The EIS company must carry on its qualifying trade for at least three years from the date it issues the EIS shares on which tax relief is claimed.

Clearly, the list of "excluded activities" means that a property company could never be an EIS company, but an EIS company may nevertheless be of interest to a property investor who has made a large capital gain by selling one or more of his properties.

Case Study - 22 EIS Deferral Relief

Gary has just sold his property portfolio for £2 million, and has made a gain (before taper relief) of £500,000.

He decides to set up a trading company that will run a pub. His Tax Adviser explains that it should be possible to set the company up in such a way that he will qualify for EIS deferral relief – although running a hotel is an "excluded activity", provided that the pub does not offer overnight accommodation it will not be within the definition of a hotel.

Gary pays his new company £500,000 and the company issues shares to him in return. Because Gary owns more than 30% of the company (in fact, he owns it all!) he cannot claim the EIS income tax relief on his subscription for the shares, but he can still claim deferral relief for his capital gain.

As Gary has invested the full amount of the gain in the EIS company, all of his capital gain is deferred – note that for the EIS it is not necessary to invest all the sale proceeds, as it is with rollover relief.

The company spends the £500,000 on acquiring a pub (it must do this within strict time limits). Provided it continues to run the pub for at least three years, Gary's deferral relief is safe.

When Gary sells the shares, the £500,000 gain he deferred becomes taxable again – though he could defer the gain once more by investing in another EIS company.

Any gain on the shares themselves will not be exempt (because he did not qualify for the income tax relief as he owned over 30% of the company), but this too could be deferred by another EIS investment.

10.2.2. *Corporate Venturing Scheme ("CVS")*

The **CVS** could be described as an EIS for companies, and it shares many of the same rules about "qualifying companies" with the EIS.

The reliefs offered by the CVS to companies that invest in new shares in a qualifying company are:

- Relief from corporation tax at 20% on the amount invested
- If the CVS shares are sold at a loss, the company may deduct that loss from its profits for the year
- When the company sells the CVS shares, it can defer any capital gain it makes on them by reinvesting in new CVS shares

The CVS reliefs are only available if the company making the investment owns less than 30% of the CVS company, so this relief is less likely to be of interest to a property business company.

11. Two Property Tax Pitfalls

In this chapter we will look at two pitfalls that the property business owner should be aware of.

One of these concerns a property investment partnership, and the other a company.

11.1. When is a Partnership Not a Partnership?

We have already seen in section 1.2 of this guide that a partnership is "persons carrying on a business in common and with a view to profit".

The Partnership Act 1890 defines a "business" as including "every trade, occupation or profession".

HMRC take the view that simply owning a property jointly with another person and receiving a share of the rent from it does not amount to an "occupation or profession", and we have already seen that it is not a trade.

They argue that in most cases, income from jointly owned property is not income from a partnership.

11.1.1. Why Does it Matter?

Given that HMRC agree that joint owners of property can agree how the income from the property is divided between them, this distinction may not seem very important.

In the case of joint owners of property who are not married, the distinction is unlikely to become relevant unless one of them is also a partner in a trading business which itself lets property, and then only if there are losses involved:

Case Study - 23 Partnerships (1)

Peter is a partner in a firm of tax advisers. The firm also owns a couple of investment properties, which it lets out. For the tax year 2006/07, the rentals from these properties produce a loss, of which Peter's share is £1,000.

Peter also owns a rental property jointly with his brother (who is also a partner in the Tax firm). During the same tax year, they make a profit on the rent from the property of £1,000 each.

Peter cannot set the loss from the partnership rents against the profit on the jointly owned property, because they are two separate property businesses.

Bigger problems can arise, however, with rental properties jointly owned by a married couple (or, ironically, a "civil partnership").

This is because there is specific legislation which allocates the income from jointly owned assets to them, as follows:

- The income is deemed to be split equally between the couple, UNLESS
- They do not in fact own equal shares of it, and they elect (using a "Form 17")
- To be taxed based on their actual ownership of it.

Case Study - 24 Partnerships (2)

Rowley and his wife Nellie jointly own a property. As we have already seen (Case Study - 20) Rowley pays income tax at 40%, but Nellie does not have any income. The rental profit from the property is £12,000 per year.

It seems sensible to the couple (who believe, wrongly, that they are a property letting partnership), to agree that the profits of the partnership should be split 10% to Rowley, and 90% to Nellie.

The tax inspector explains to them that in his opinion their property letting is not a partnership, because it does not involve sufficient business activity on their part – it is essentially a passive investment.

After some argument, they reluctantly accept his view, but Nellie asks why it is so important, given that HMRC accept that joint owners can agree how to divide the income from their property.

The inspector explains that this does not apply to married couples, and runs through the rules referred to above. Because the income from the jointly owned property must be split equally between them, the result is:

	Rowley	**Nellie**	**Total**
Rental split as "partnership"	1,200	10,800	12,000
Tax due	480	959	1,439
Rental split 50:50	6,000	6,000	12,000
Tax due	2,400	78	2,478

As a result of splitting the income in the correct way, the couple are paying over £1,000 more income tax.

What could they do?

For the future, they could change their ownership of the property, by converting their joint ownership into a "tenancy in common" (a simple legal procedure), and Rowley could then give 4/5 of his half share to Nellie (there is no CGT on gifts between spouses).

They would then own the property in a 90:10 proportion, and they can now submit a Form 17 to the inspector, but the new split of the income will only apply from the date they make this "declaration".

Note that if there is a mortgage on the property, then a gift between spouses may give rise to a charge to Stamp Duty Land Tax (SDLT), and even if it does not, the gift must be notified to HMRC on Form SDLT1.

Case Study - 25 Partnerships and Stamp Duty

A husband owns a buy to let property valued at £300,000, on which he has secured a mortgage of £240,000. He makes a gift of the property (still encumbered with the mortgage), to his wife.

Although the wife did not pay anything for the property, she has taken over liability for the £240,000 mortgage, so she must pay SDLT at 1% = £2,400.

If instead the husband had only given her a half share in the property, she would be treated as having taken over half the mortgage - £120,000.

This is below the threshold for SDLT, so there is no duty to pay, but HMRC must be notified about the transaction (using Form SDLT 1).

11.2. How Limited is Your Liability?

One of the advantages of a company over a sole tradership or a partnership is said to be the fact that the shareholder's liability is "limited" – see section 1.3 of this guide.

This is true as far as it goes, but in the real world, this "limited liability" can be an illusion.

A company needs cash. When it first starts its business life, it can only raise that cash from one of two sources:

- By issuing shares in exchange for cash
- By borrowing money

The cash shareholders put into the company when they subscribe for shares is, of course, at risk if things go wrong – "limited liability" means that at worst they will lose this money.

When a company borrows money, it can either borrow it from:

- Its shareholders, or
- Commercial lenders – such as banks

Clearly, if the money is borrowed from the shareholders, they are also at risk for that money if things go wrong (and note that if their company is in difficulties, there are strict rules against repaying the shareholders' loans in preference to the company's other debts).

If the company borrows from a commercial lender (say, a bank), particularly when it is a fairly new company, it is extremely likely that the bank will demand a "personal guarantee" from one or more of the shareholders/directors.

A "personal guarantee" (known as a "PG") is a promise from the individual concerned that if the company fails to repay the money it has borrowed, then the individual will step in and repay the loan himself.

Typically, a PG will be backed up by a "charge" on the individual's other property – most typically, his home. A "charge" means that if the individual fails to repay the loan after the company defaults, then the bank can take his home and sell it to get its money back.

In many cases, therefore, the limited liability offered by a company will not be as good a protection as it may appear at first sight:

Case Study - 26 Limited Liability

Andrew sets up a company to develop a property. The company needs £250,000 to buy the property and to renovate it and sell it. The money comes from:

- Andrew's subscription for shares - £10,000
- Loan from Andrew (his life savings) - £40,000
- Loan from High Street Bank (with a PG from Andrew) - £200,000

The company buys the land and begins to develop it, but unfortunately discovers that there are old mine workings undermining the entire property.

Building cannot continue, and the land is sold off at a knock-down price (being virtually useless for anything). When the dust settles, the company's assets are £100,000 in cash.

Because the £100,000 is not enough to repay the bank, they call in Andrew's PG (which is secured on his house), and he has to sell this in order to pay the

£100,000 owed to the bank after it has taken all the company's cash.

Andrew also loses the £40,000 he had lent to the company, and his £10,000 worth of shares are now worth nothing.

Andrew does not feel that his limited liability as a shareholder has been much help to him!

In certain other circumstances, a director may become liable for the company's debts even though he has not lent it any money and given no PGs.

If a director allows a company to continue in business when he knows (**or should have known)** that the company will not be able to pay its debts, then he can be sued for "wrongful trading", and can be required to provide funds to help the company pay off its creditors.

For this reason, directors whose companies are getting into financial trouble should not ignore the problem. They should seek their accountant's advice immediately, in order to avoid the risk of becoming personally liable if the company goes under.

12. Close Companies

All of the companies featured in the case studies in this guide are "close" companies. In this chapter we will become more familiar with this terminology and understand how it can be used.

12.1. What is a Close Company?

A "close" company is a company which is controlled by:

- Five or fewer "participators", or
- Any number of "participators", if those "participators" are directors

A "participator", broadly, means a shareholder.

Case Study - 27 Examples of Close Companies

Example of "close" companies include:

- The shares in Company A are owned equally by three individuals. Company A is a close company, because it is controlled by five or fewer participators
- The shares in Company B are owned equally by 9 individuals. Company B is a close company, because any 5 of the 9 could control it
- The shares in company C are owned equally by 5 married couples. Company C is a close company, because when looking at "control" you include shares held by "associates" and married couples are associates of each other.

This is only a very broad summary of the rules defining a close company, because the detailed rules are extremely complicated, being designed to prevent people artificially creating a company which should be a close company but is not.

For the purposes of this guide, assume that any property investment or property development company you set up is going to be a close company.

12.2. Special Rules for Close Companies

There are certain special rules for close companies, which cover:

- The meaning of a "distribution" from the close company

- The tax on loans from the close company to its participators
- The way corporation tax is calculated for certain types of close company

12.3. The Meaning of a "Distribution" From a Close Company

If a close company provides any "benefits or facilities of whatever nature" to a participator (or his associates) in a close company, then this is treated as if the company had paid him a dividend equivalent to the benefit.

This does not apply if the participator is also a director or employee of the company, because then the benefit will be charged to income tax as part of his remuneration from the company. It is therefore quite unusual to come across this sort of situation:

Case Study - 28 Distribution to a Participator

Closeco Ltd is a close company, and one of the shareholders is Daniel. Daniel is not a director and does not work for the company, and is not related to any of the other shareholders. The company manufactures TV sets, and one Christmas, it gives each of its shareholders a brand new plasma TV.

Most of the shareholders are directors of the company and so they are taxed on the TVs as a benefit in kind from their employment, but Daniel is not, so he is treated as if he had received a dividend equivalent to the cost to the company of the TV.

If the cost of the TV is £1,000, then Daniel (a higher rate taxpayer) will be charged to income tax of £250.

The company was able to claim a deduction for the cost of the TVs supplied to the directors (as a cost of employing them), but it cannot get a deduction for the cost of Daniel's TV.

12.4. Loan to a Participator

Much more common is a **loan to a participator**.
This will occur if the company lends money to one of its shareholders. The company will be required to pay tax under section 419 ICTA 1988 on the amount of the loan. The rate of tax is 25% of the amount of the loan.

16.8 When the loan is repaid, the tax will be refunded. The timing of this is important.

Case Study - 29 Section 419 Tax

A close company makes a loan of £10,000 to a shareholder. When it puts in its corporation tax return (which must be within nine months after its year end), it must include section 419 tax of £2,500 in its tax payment – unless the loan was repaid within nine months of the end of the accounting period, in which case no section 419 tax is due.

Assuming the loan was not repaid within nine months of the end of the accounting period in which it was made, then the section 419 tax will only be repaid nine months after the end of the accounting period in which the loan is repaid.

For example:
The company prepares its accounts for the calendar year, and on 31 December 2001 it lends £10,000 to a shareholder. The loan is repaid on 1 January 2003.

On 1 October 2002, the company pays its corporation tax for the 2001 year, and section 419 tax of £2,500.

On 1 October 2003, the company pays its corporation tax for the 2002 year. It cannot claim back the section 419 tax, because although the loan has been repaid by now, it was repaid after the end of the 2002 accounting year.

On 1 October 2004, the company pays its corporation tax for the 2003 year, and because it is now nine months after the end of the accounting period in which the loan was repaid, it can claim repayment of the section 419 tax.

Although the loan was only outstanding for one year and two days, the section 419 tax is not repaid until two years after it was paid.

Some companies try to get round this by "bed and breakfasting" the loan:
The company makes up its accounts to the calendar year. On 1 January 2004, it lends £40,000 to a shareholder.

On 30 December 2004, the shareholder borrows £40,000 from his rich uncle, and repays the loan.

On 2 January 2005, he again borrows £40,000 from the company, and repays his uncle.

On 30 December 2005, he borrows £40,000 from uncle….. and so on!

Because the loan never appears in the company's balance sheet at 31 December, the company believes there is no section 419 tax to pay – after all, the loan has been repaid, hasn't it?

HMRC take the view that a temporary repayment of a loan in this way is not effective – in fact they go further, and say that it is bordering on fraud!

It is very unwise for a company to rely on "bed and breakfasting" a loan in this way.

In order to get the section 419 tax repaid, the company can also write off the loan. In other words, the company formally declares that it will cancel the loan. The tax consequences of this are:

- The company can claim repayment of the section 419 tax as if the loan had been repaid (or if the loan is written off within 9 months of the accounting period in which it was made, no section 419 tax will be due).

- The shareholder is taxed as if he had received a dividend equal to the loan being written off.

This can be used as a planning tool:

Case Study - 30 Write off of a Loan

In Case Study 11, we saw the problems that can arise if a company pays dividends to its shareholders that are not proportionate to their shareholdings. If instead of paying a dividend to the shareholders, the company lent them money and then wrote off the loan, they would get the same tax effect as a dividend.

The timing of the tax payment can be better, as well.

Compare the timing of the tax payment between a dividend and a loan written off:

The company makes up its accounts to the calendar year.

In scenario A, it pays a dividend of £5,000 on 6 April 2005 to a shareholder, who pays income tax at the higher rate..

In scenario B, it lends £5,000 to the same shareholder, also on 6 April 2005. It then writes the loan off on 6 April 2006.

In scenario A, the shareholder has received a dividend in the tax year 2005/06. He will be liable to pay income tax of £1,250 by 31 January 2007.

In scenario B, the shareholder has received a distribution in the tax year 2006/07 (the tax year in which the loan was written off). He will be liable to pay the same amount of income tax (£1,250), but not until 31 January 2008.

Because the loan was written off within 9 months of the end of the accounting year in which it was made, the company does not have to pay any section 419 tax.

In both scenarios, the shareholder has had the use of the money from 6 April 2005, but the date on which he has to pay income tax on it has been deferred by a year.

Caution

This particular planning technique is not as simple as it appears, and you should take advice from a tax consultant before using it. There are a number of aspects of company law to consider, and also the "preordained series of transactions" rules we have already looked at – see Case Study - 15.

There is one more special rule for close companies that we need to consider – the taxation of "**Close Investment Holding" Companies.**

We have seen that companies pay corporation tax at only 20% on their profits up to £300,000 per year – see Part 6. This does not apply to a "Close Investment Holding Company" ("CIC").

A CIC pays corporation tax on ALL its profits at 30%.

12.5. What is a CIC?

Like many definitions in taxation, a CIC is defined by exclusion. In other words, ALL close companies are CICs, except for those which exist "wholly or mainly" for the following purposes:

- Trading
- Letting property to unconnected third parties
- Being part of a group of companies engaged in the above activities

The test of whether a company is a CIC is applied at the END of its accounting period. If it is a CIC at the end of its accounting period, it pays the 30% rate of corporation tax on its profits **for the whole of that accounting period**.

This can lead to problems. Consider the following scenario:

Case Study - 31 The Accidental CIC

Property Co Ltd is a close company. It owns three investment properties, and makes up its accounts to the calendar year.

Between April and July in 2006, it sells off its three investment properties.

The cash from these sales is held on deposit at the bank. The plan is to liquidate the company, but its directors are busy people, and things just drift on until the liquidation begins on 1 February 2007, after the company's year end on 31 December 2006.

The company's profits for the year 2006 are:

Rents received before Sale of properties	10,000
Gains on sale of properties	300,000
Bank interest	10,000
Total profits	320,000

The company expects to pay corporation tax of:

First 300,000 at 20%	60,000
20,000 at 32.5%	6,500
Total	66,500
Rate of CT	20.78%

Unfortunately, after the company sold its last property in July 2006, its only source of income was bank interest on the cash it had received.

Unless the company can show that at 31 December 2006 it had the intention of investing the cash in more properties (which would be difficult, considering it was put into liquidation one month later), or in a trading activity, at the end of its accounting period on 31 December 2006, it was a CIC.

A CIC pays corporation tax at 30% on all its profits, so the CT due on £320,000 would be £96,000 – an increase of £29,500 on what it had expected to pay.

There are various things that can be done to avoid the CIC problem in these circumstances:

- Shortening the company's accounting period
- Early commencement of liquidation
- Postponing the decision to liquidate

The choice between these alternatives can be a very difficult one, and where a company is coming to the point where it is going to sell its last investment property (or stop trading as a property developer) and liquidate, it is ESSENTIAL to get expert tax advice BEFORE the last property is sold or the trade ceases.

13. The Directors' Tax Liabilities

So far, we have looked only at the tax directors of a company will pay on salaries and dividends.

This chapter considers the other tax liabilities they may have in relation to the company.

13.1. Tax on Non-Cash Benefits

Directors (and any other employee of a company earning over £8,500 per year) are liable to tax on non-cash benefits they receive from the company that employs them. Even employees earning less than £8,500 per year are liable to tax on certain specified benefits.

The whole area of employee benefits is a complex and specialised branch of tax, but this chapter attempts to give some guidelines on the pitfalls to avoid, and one or two opportunities as well.

Directors are also liable to tax on any business expenses the company reimburses to them, though they can make a claim in their own tax return for a deduction for those same expenses.

We will deal with expenses first.

13.2. Expenses

Directors may incur expenses when on the company's business. The most common example is travelling expenses.

13.2.1. Travelling expenses

The cost of business travel is an allowable expense, subject to certain exclusions. The one that most commonly causes problems is travel from home to work.

Travel from your home to your normal place of work is "ordinary commuting" and the cost is not allowable as a business expense. This can be a particular problem for the typical small family company.

If the company has a headquarters, such as a rented office in a town, or a yard where it keeps its building equipment, then travel from home to that place is unlikely to be an allowable expense.

If, on the other hand, the company's base of operations is the home of the controlling director, travel from his home to anywhere where the company's business is being conducted – such as a building site, or a property being refurbished – is an allowable expense.

If a property investment company uses a letting agent to administer the properties it lets, then it is likely that HMRC will argue that the business is being administered through the agent, and that therefore the director's home is just a home, and not where the company's business is carried on, even if he brings paperwork home occasionally.

Any company whose directors are incurring significant travelling expenses should check with a tax adviser to confirm that the expenses are allowable – getting it wrong can be expensive, as we shall see in chapter 14, which deals with tax investigations.

13.2.2. Cars

Most travelling expenses involve the cost of running a car.

It used to be a good tax planning idea to have the company own a car, and allow the director to use it for both business and private purposes, as the rules for taxing directors on their private use of a "company car" were very generous.

These rules have been made progressively more punitive over the years, and it is now very unlikely that it will be beneficial for a director who also owns the company to have a company car.

There is no substitute for doing the figures for the individual director and car, but it nearly always turns out that he will be better off owning the car privately and charging the company for his business mileage.

13.2.3. Using Your Own Car for Business

A director who uses his own car for business mileage can be reimbursed tax free by the company at a rate of 40p per mile for the first 10,000 business miles in the tax year (year to 5 April), and at 25p per mile for any further business mileage.

Note that this is the only reimbursement that is allowable for tax purposes. If the director claims the actual cost of his business mileage – by keeping records of all running costs and of his business and private mileage – then when the company pays him for these expenses, the payment is taxable.

The director can make a claim in his tax return for the 40p per mile mileage allowance, but he will have to pay tax on the payments from the company.

13.2.4. Using Cars for Sole Traders and Partnerships

By contrast, the sole trader or partner in a property business needs to keep full records and claim the actual cost of the business miles. For a trader, provided the turnover of the business is below the VAT threshold (£64,000 from 1 April 2007), the 40p/25p method can be used instead if he wishes. Strictly, this does not apply to a property letting business (because it is not a trade), though where the turnover is below £64,000, some inspectors will accept this method.

13.2.5. Three Important Differences to Remember

This is an excellent example of three important differences between the tax treatment of companies and their directors as compared to sole traders/partners:

- The relationship between a company and its director is more formal than that between a sole trader/partner and his business
- The rules for directors tend to be restrictive and punitive compared to sole traders
- The differences between the two sets of rules defy common sense!

13.3. Other Expenses

Motoring expenses, providing the rules described above are followed, are not taxable on directors, but most other expenses are – for example:

- The company pays the director's train fare to visit a development site where the company is building some buy to sell properties
- The director has to attend a meeting to close a deal on a new property, and because it is a long journey from his home, the company reimburses him for the cost of an overnight stay in a hotel
- The director uses his own credit card to pay for goods or services for the company, and claims the cost back from the company

Golden Rule

In all the above cases, the expenses payments to the director are taxable.

They must either be reported on the annual return by the company of benefits provided to a director (known as a Form P11D), or in the case of cash payments, they should strictly be paid under deduction of PAYE. The director can then make a claim in his own tax return for the same expenses, and if they meet the rules for allowable expenses, he will be allowed a deduction for them – he may even, eventually, get a tax repayment as a result.

Fortunately, it is possible to shortcut this process, by getting a formal **dispensation** from HMRC.

13.4. Dispensations

A dispensation is a notice signed by a tax inspector to say that he is satisfied that the types of expenses listed in the dispensation are ones that the director could successfully claim a deduction for.

Once the dispensation is in place, the company can pay or reimburse the expenses listed in the dispensation without having to report them as taxable benefits.

> **Caution**
>
> It must be stressed that only if a dispensation is in place can the company and the director avoid the merry-go-round of the company reporting the expenses payments as taxable and the director then claiming them back in his tax return. This is a favourite target in certain types of tax investigation – see the next chapter of this guide.

13.5. Shares as Rewards

We have seen how the company is owned by its shareholders, and how their shares entitle them to their proportion of dividends paid and, ultimately, to a share of the company's assets when it is wound up. For many years, shares have also been used as a way of providing benefits to employees, and in some cases as a way of trying to pay them in a way that escaped tax and NIC, or reduced their impact.

As a result, HMRC and the Treasury have introduced more and more complex and punitive rules taxing employees and directors on the benefit of any "employment related securities" they are given.

This is not the place for a detailed examination of these rules (that would take a book longer than the whole of this one) but the following Case Study illustrates the type of pitfall to watch out for.

> **Case Study - 32 Shares as Rewards**
>
> Mr Fox and Mr Hound both own very similar property development companies. They are both the sole shareholders, and they are both getting on in years.
>
> Mr Fox has two sons, who both work in the business, and he decides he would like to give them 24% of his shares each – Mr Fox is a great family man, and says he believes in "keeping the family business within the family". He will still have 52% of the shares, but if all goes well over the next few years, he will be able to hand over full control and enjoy a well-earned retirement.
>
> Mr Hound is in exactly the same situation and has exactly the same plans, except that in his case he has only one daughter, and no sons. He does, however, have a very loyal manager (not related to him, and though on good terms with the family, not an intimate friend), who has worked for the company for many years, and who could be trusted to help his daughter in running the company – "she is a good buyer of land, and he is an excellent project manager", he explains. Mr Hound does exactly the same as Mr Fox – he gives 24% of his shares to each of his daughter and the manager, with a view to handing over to them entirely in a few years if all goes well.
>
> Because Foxco Ltd and Houndco Ltd are both trading companies, Mr Fox and

Mr Hound can "hold over" the capital gains tax on their disposals of their shares – which is just as well, because the shares are now worth several hundreds of thousands of pounds – both companies are doing well and have a number of profitable projects on the go.

The tax treatment of the recipients of the shares is very different, though.

In the Fox brothers' case, HMRC will probably accept that the gift of the shares is covered by the ONLY exception to the rules for "employment related securities", which excludes shares given to employees "in the normal course of the domestic, family, or personal relationships" of the person giving them.

There are no income tax implications for the Fox boys.

Miss Hound and the manager, however, are in a very different position. Because Miss Hound received her shares at the same time as the (unrelated) manager, it is virtually impossible to argue that hers were "domestic, family, or personal relationships" shares.

It certainly cannot be argued that the manager's shares were not in some way related to his job.

You will also notice that Mr Fox was careful to stress the importance of family, and to keep his mouth shut about the obvious fact that he hoped the boys would be motivated to put more effort into the company once they owned a large slice of it, whereas Mr Hound could not resist mentioning what a good job the manager and his daughter were doing.

As a result, Miss Hound and the manager will be liable to income tax on the market value (hundreds of thousands of pounds, remember!) of the shares they have been given, and in the particular circumstances of this case, there will very probably be a PAYE and NIC liability, which Houndco will have to pay, and then further tax liabilities if Miss Hound and the manager do not reimburse the company for that tax and NIC.

If you think the distinction between the way the two companies were treated is exaggerated, please note that both Foxco and Houndco are based on two real cases I have dealt with – though in the case of Houndco, I am glad to say that the real Mr Hound spoke to me before making the gifts of shares and we were able to avert a disaster by changing the arrangements.

It is never safe to assume that if an employee or director (or their close family) acquires shares in the company he works for, there will be no tax implications.

Even if you acquire your shares as a result of setting up your own new company, it is probable that the company will be required to report the fact (on a "Form 42", by 7 July after the end of the tax year in which you acquired the shares). There are some narrow exceptions to this rule, but they are very narrow exceptions.

Always ask your Tax Adviser **before** you enter into **any** transaction involving shares and employees – this is a complicated and dangerous area, but to look on the bright side, there is much that can be done to reduce the tax burdens involved.

13.6. FOUR Tax Free Benefits

To end this Part on a more cheerful note, let us look at a few benefits that a company can provide to its directors without any tax liability arising.

The tax free benefits provided below may seem trivial, but their value mounts up.

Car parking
The company can provide any employee with a car parking space at or near his place of work (either in the company's own car park, or in a commercial car park).

Mobile phones
The company can provide a mobile phone – though since April 2006, this has been restricted to one phone per employee.

Child Care
The company can pay for childcare (in a commercial nursery or with an approved childminder) for employees' children, up to a maximum of £50 per week per employee, free of tax. Note that this benefit must be offered to all employees, whereas the benefits mentioned previously may be offered selectively.

Meals
Provided they are available to all employees, free meals in a works canteen or in the business premises (e.g. sandwich lunches) are tax free, provided they are "on a reasonable scale" (so no caviar sandwiches!). Note that the exemption does not apply to meals in cafes, restaurants, or pubs.

Case Study - 33 Tax Free Benefits

Mr and Mrs Laurel have a property company. They are the directors, and there are no employees.

The company provides them with the following benefits:

- A parking space each (they have two cars, and often one of them needs to go off alone, to visit a site for example) in the multi-storey near the company's office. The cost is £30 per week each

- A mobile phone each – cost £25 per month each

- Childcare for their two-year-old twins – cost £50 per week each

- Sandwich lunches eaten at their desks when they are in the office – cost £35 per week

The total yearly cost of these benefits is £9,375 (based on 45 working weeks in the year).

The company gets a tax deduction for all these costs, so the actual cost is only £7,500 after taking account of the tax relief in the company.

Mr and Mrs Hardy have a similar company, and incur all the same expenses as those above, but they pay for them out of their (taxed) income because they wrongly assume they would have to pay tax on benefits in kind if the company provided them.

In order to have £9,375 to spend on these expenses, they need to draw dividends of that amount from the company, on which they pay tax at 25%, so the total cost is £12,500 (remember, the company does not get a deduction for the cost of a dividend).

By using the company to pay expenses they would have incurred anyway, the Laurels have saved £5,000.

14. Companies and Tax Investigations

HMRC have the power to "enquire" into any tax return from a company, a partnership, or an individual. They do not have to give a reason for the enquiry.

These "enquiries" come in several different forms, and this Part concentrates on the types of enquiry a company may face.

A sole trader or partnership is just as likely to face an enquiry, but as we shall see in this chapter, there are certain special features when a company is involved.

14.1. "Aspect" Enquiries

These are the least serious type of Enquiry – though they have been known to develop into "Full Enquiries" as they progress.

In an Aspect Enquiry, the inspector will ask questions about a specific issue in the return – a favourite example for a property company would be to check if amounts claimed for repairs to a let property are in fact improvements to it (which cannot be deducted from rental income).

Most Aspect Enquiries are closed down with no penalties being charged – though this is not always the case if large or blatant errors are found – but there will be interest to pay on any additional tax that is collected, running from the date the tax would have been paid if the return had been correct in the first place.

14.2. "Compliance" Enquiries

This is my term for Enquiries aimed at checking that the business has complied with its obligations under the various laws and regulations it is obliged to obey. For property businesses, the commonest are:

- **Construction Industry Scheme (CIS) compliance**
  The CIS applies to all property developers (but not to property investors), and requires them to check the credentials of all the subcontractors they use, and record all payments to them, while in some cases deducting tax from those payments.

  See my other guide "**Tax Secrets for Property Developers and Renovators**" for more details of the CIS and the procedure for HMRC checks on compliance.

- **PAYE and benefits in kind**
  A sole trader or partnership will only be liable to this type of Enquiry if it has employees, but ANY company could face one – because its directors are employees for tax purposes.

  The Enquiry will check if the company has operated PAYE correctly, and if all benefits in kind and expenses payments have been correctly reported on the annual Forms P11D.

- **VAT**
  HMRC will check that any property purchases have been handled correctly regarding the Transfer of a Going Concern issues and that options to tax have been in place properly on commercial buildings.

14.3. Full Enquiry

This is the type of Enquiry that is generally referred to as a Tax Investigation, and it will involve the inspector looking at all the business accounts and records, and in some cases the private bank statements, etc., of the owners or directors. It may also involve some or all of the more specialised types of Enquiry referred to above.

This is not the place for a detailed examination of how to deal with a tax investigation, but there is one vital piece of advice – **do not attempt to deal with it yourself!** In particular, if you or your company receive a notice from the tax inspector to say he has decided to "Enquire" into your or your company's return, **seek professional help immediately** – in the first instance, from your accountant, though in serious cases he may well want to call in a tax specialist like me.

There are two specific problem areas in investigations that are peculiar to companies (though the first could also apply to a sole trader or partnership if they had employees):

14.4. "Grossing up"

Where an employee (including a director) has received payments that should have been made under PAYE, the inspector will generally argue that the tax liability should be settled by the employer rather than the employee, and that this should be done by "grossing up" the payments made.

Case Study - 34 Grossing Up

A company has paid a weekly cash sum of £50 to its directors to cover "general expenses". It is agreed that this should have been paid under PAYE.

The directors are higher rate taxpayers, so for each director to have received £50 in cash, the PAYE deductions would have been:

Gross payment	**84.75**
Less income tax at 40%	**(33.90)**
Less employee's NIC at 1%	**(0.85)**
Gives weekly cash	**50**

In addition, the company would have had to pay employers NIC at 12.8% on the £84.75 – another £10.85.

So, for each director involved, the annual amount of tax and NIC the inspector will seek to claim will be:

Weekly income tax	33.90
Weekly employee NIC	0.85
Weekly employer's NIC	10.85
Weekly total	45.60
Times 53 gives	2,416

(Note – the PAYE year is often 53 weeks long, and also note it is HMRC practice to round down to the nearest pound!)

"Grossing up" does not always happen – but it is almost always the position HMRC start from, and you will need a Tax Adviser who has experience of negotiating with HMRC on these cases to ensure the damage is limited as much as possible.

14.5. Company Investigation Settlements

Company Investigation Settlements are also complicated by the way that companies and their directors are regarded by HMRC when it is found that tax has been lost, particularly as a result of undeclared income.

Case Study - 35 Undeclared Income in a Company

Mr Burke is a sole trader, and when his return and accounts are investigated, it is found that he has failed to include £10,000 income for the year – the rent from a property he owns.

The inspector explains that Mr Burke should have paid £4,000 income tax on this income, and so Mr Burke will have to pay:

Tax	4,000

Penalties at 25% of tax (see later in this Part)	1,000
Total	5,200
Rounded up to	5,500

(in reality, it is also likely that the £10,000 would be "scaled back" to the previous six years, using the Retail Price Index to estimate how much was missing in those years, but I have ignored this for the sake of simplicity)

Mr Burke agrees to this, pays up, and that is the end of the matter.

Mr Hare is the sold shareholder and director of a company, and it is found that £10,000 rental income has gone missing from his company's accounts and found its way into his pocket.

The tax consequences are more complicated, because HMRC take the view that sums "misappropriated" by directors are loans to them from the company.

This means that:

- The company has "lent" Mr Hare £10,000, and HMRC will insist that he pays it back as a condition of settling the Enquiry. If Mr Hare does not have the money, then the company may have to pay him a dividend to fund the repayment – income tax for Mr Hare of £2,500.
- The company owes section 419 tax (see Case Study 28) of £2,500. Although this will be repaid when Mr Hare repays the "loan", the company will still have to pay interest in it from the date it should have paid it.
- By lending the money interest free to Mr Hare, the company has given him a benefit in kind, and he will have to pay income tax based on the official rate of interest (currently 6.25%, so Mr Hare is taxed on a benefit of £625) – but this normally only runs from the date he agrees that the cash has been misappropriated until the day he repays it.
- The company should have paid corporation tax at 20% on the £10,000, so it owes £2,000.
- As with Mr Burke, there will be interest and penalties on all this.

I have not offered a total of Mr Hare's and his company's casts, because these are so much a matter for negotiation with HMRC that any figure I gave would be misleading.

Note also that the "scaling back" to earlier years referred to with Mr Burke will apply here as well, so the amount Mr Hare will have to repay to the company could be very large indeed.

I have mentioned penalties, and it is important to understand how these are calculated, because it is possible to reduce them if the investigation is properly handled.

Penalty calculations start from the amount of the tax that has been wrongly underpaid – this is the maximum possible penalty.

This maximum is then "mitigated" according to a formula:

	Maximum mitigation
Disclosure	20% (25% in special cases)
Co-operation	40%
Size and gravity	40%
Total	100%

14.6. Disclosure

Disclosure refers to whether the taxpayer "owned up" to the tax irregularities, or whether he denied everything until he could no longer think of any more excuses. Broadly, a taxpayer who "puts his hands up" and admits everything immediately the enquiry begins will get 20%.

At the other extreme, the taxpayer who denies and denies, perhaps forcing HMRC to go to the Tax Commissioners – an independent tribunal that decides disputes between HMRC and taxpayers – would get 0%. The "extra" 5% to make up 25% is only for a taxpayer who voluntarily approaches HMRC and confesses, and then only if he "has no reason to fear discovery".

Unfortunately, this does not mean you can get a repayment of 5% - the extra 5% is used to mitigate the penalties under the other two headings!

14.7. Co-operation

Co-operation – this is fairly self-explanatory, and is why you should never drag your feet during an investigation, but you will need a good tax adviser to help you understand the difference between lack of co-operation and insisting on fair treatment and arguing technical issues.

14.8. Size and Gravity

Size and Gravity – this seems to cause the most arguments in settlement negotiations. The mitigation ranges from 40% for cases of muddle and mistake involving small sums, to (theoretically) 0% for serious fraud involving forgery, conspiracy and large sums of tax – though at this end of the scale, it is more likely that there would be a criminal prosecution. A Tax Adviser will be particularly on his guard with an inexperienced inspector here – they always seem to think that their investigation targets are more "heinous" than anyone else's!

If we go back to Mr Burke in Case Study - 35:

Case Study - 36 Penalty Calculation

Mr Burke had concealed £10,000 income (by not declaring rent he received from a property). The mitigation of his penalties was agreed as:

Disclosure 15% - Mr Burke initially denied it all, but quickly realised this was stupid and admitted he had been receiving the rent

Co-operation 30% - Having admitted to the rents, Mr Burke quickly produced a schedule showing the amounts and dates, which proved to be an accurate one when the inspector checked it. However, he also tried to make a claim for some repairs, but had to withdraw this when he could not produce any invoices

Size and Gravity 30% - Mr Burke simply did not include the rent in his return – he did not produce any false documents, no-one else was involved, and the money was not hidden in offshore accounts or anything of that sort. On the other hand, £10,000 is a lot of money and it is clear he deliberately did not declare it even though he knew he should have done.

The total of Mr Burke's mitigation was 75%, and that is why the penalty was 25% as shown in Case Study 34.

14.9. Watch out for the COP 9

There is one other kind of investigation to consider. This is where HMRC believe there has been serious tax fraud. In these cases, they will ask for a meeting under **Code of Practice 9 ("COP 9").**

If you are ever called in for a COP 9 meeting, it is **ABSOLUTELY ESSENTIAL** to take expert advice from a suitably experienced Tax Adviser before attending it, and to be accompanied by that adviser to the meeting. UNDER NO CIRCUMSTANCES try to handle this yourself, and, at the risk of offending the profession, it is unlikely that your regular accountant will have the expertise to deal with a COP 9 investigation.

14.10. Four Golden Rules of Tax Investigations

To end this part, here are the golden rules for dealing with tax enquiries:

- DON'T try to handle it yourself – get advice before you reply to the initial letter from the inspector, and at all costs DON'T ring the inspector up to "have a chat and sort this out"

- DON'T ignore it and hope it will go away – remember the mitigation of penalties for co-operation and disclosure

- DO be honest and upfront with your Tax Adviser – only then will he be able to help you

- DO talk to your accountant about taking out insurance to cover the fees for a tax investigation – the professional fees can be very expensive

Note – The 2007 Budget announced changes to the penalty regime for tax investigations. These are likely to be implemented for the 2008/09 tax year, and at the time of writing (April 2007) the details have not yet been published, but one thing looks certain – the penalties under the new rules will be significantly higher than under the present regime.

15. Getting Your "Tax" Exit Strategy Right

It seems appropriate to include this towards the end of this guide, but in fact, you should be thinking about your proposed exit route from the first day you start your business, as it may affect how you set it up and the strategic decisions you make as time goes on.

15.1. Everybody Has an Exit Strategy

Some businessmen say they have no exit route – they will work till they drop, and leave the business to their children – but that is itself an exit route, and one we shall consider further in chapter 16.

15.2. The THREE Most Common Exit Strategies

If you decide not to leave the business to your children then it is highly likely you will adopt one of the following three possible exit routes:

- Sell the business as a going concern
- Liquidate the business and invest the cash in something else
- Keep the business as a source of retirement income

15.3. Selling the Business

For the sole trader or partner, there is little distinction between selling the business as a going concern, and simply selling off the business assets. In either case, he will pay capital gains tax on the gain he makes from the sale of the business assets, and his main concern will be whether or not he gets business asset taper relief (see chapter 9).

For a company, there will be a choice to make between:

- Selling the shares in the company
- The company sells its assets and the cash is then extracted from the company

It often happens that the decision is made for the company, because the purchaser insists either on buying the shares, or on buying the assets.

A purchaser will probably be thinking along these lines:

15.3.1. Benefits of Buying the Shares in the Company

- Simplicity – the company is already up and running and all he has to do is take it over. If the business name is important, buying the company is the simplest way to acquire the name (though this can be managed in other ways if assets are purchased).

- Stamp Duty – there is a flat rate of 0.5% for purchases of shares, whereas the Stamp Duty Land Tax on the purchase of land and property can be as high as 4%.

- Financing – particularly if the purchaser is a listed company, it can offer its own shares in exchange for the shares in the business – more on this later.

15.3.2. Drawbacks of Buying the Shares in the Company

- History - when you buy a company's shares, you buy its history, including any skeletons it may have in its closet – for example, if the company has been getting its PAYE wrong, the problem will become yours once you own the shares, including any liabilities for years before you bought it.

  It is for this reason that Sale Agreements for companies tend to be more complicated than those for business assets alone, because they will (or should!) contain complex "warranties" (essentially, promises by the vendor that the company has no skeletons in the closet) and "indemnities" (promises by the vendor to pay for the funerals of any skeletons that do turn up after all!).

- Tax – in some circumstances, the purchaser may be able to get more tax reliefs for his purchase if he buys assets rather than the company – to take only one example, if a company buys business assets (not shares in a company) that include goodwill, the company may be able to get a tax deduction for the cost of the goodwill.

- Structure – if the purchaser already has a company, he may not want to buy another ("associated companies" – see Part 6) and if he does not already have a company, he may not want to run the business as a company.

From the vendor's point of view, there is a different set of considerations:

15.3.3. Benefits of Selling the Shares in the Company

- "Clean break" – by selling the company, he gets rid of its history – though this is subject to the warranties and indemnities he will probably have to give.

- CGT – especially if the shares qualify for business asset taper relief, it is likely that he will pay less tax than if the company (which cannot claim any taper relief) sells the assets.

- Double taxation – assuming the vendor wants the cash for himself, there is a "double whammy" if the company sells its business and is then liquidated, because the company will pay tax on the capital gains it makes on the sale of the assets, and then there will be another tax cost in extracting the assets from the company.

- Taper problems – if the company sells its business assets, there will often be a delay between the sale of the assets and the liquidation of the company. In some cases, this can be quite a long delay, and during this period the company will not qualify for business asset taper relief, even if it did before the sale.

- Close Investment Holding Company status after the sale – see chapter 12 for an explanation of this problem .

15.3.4. Benefits of Selling the Company's Assets and then Liquidating

I am tempted to say, "none", but it is always worth working the numbers for each individual case just to make sure.

The most common reason for asset sales is that the purchaser insists on it

15.4. Selling the Company's Shares

Sale of company's shares. The basic proposition is quite simple – the shareholder(s) of the company sell their shares, and they make a capital gain based on the difference between the price they sell for and the cost of those shares when they subscribed for them (typically very low – maybe even £1), or otherwise acquired them.

If the company is a trading company, they will get business asset taper relief, and the effective rate of tax they pay on the sale may be as low as 10% (see chapter 9); otherwise (as with a property investment company), they will only get ordinary taper relief, but even this can reduce their effective rate of tax to 24% if they have owned the company for 10 years.

The reality, of course, is much more complicated, and it is essential to bring in a Tax Adviser at an early stage in all but the very simplest of company sales.

It is impossible to set out the "correct" strategy for selling a company.

Each of the many company sales I have advised on has had its own unique features, opportunities, and problems.

What follows are some examples of the kinds of situations that commonly arise:

15.4.1. "Earn-outs"

These are a very common feature of company sales. Essentially, the shares are sold for a cash sum up front, and with the promise of more cash depending on the company's performance over, say, the next three years. Points to consider with "earn-outs" include:

- Taxation of the earn-out. This can be complicated. If the deferred payments are fixed, but subject to some condition – such as "£100,000 on 31 March 2008, and £100,000 on 31 March 2009, provided the company's profits are at least £250,000 for the next two years", then for tax purposes the vendor will be treated as receiving the **whole sum on the day he sells the company** .

  There are provisions for the CGT to be paid by instalments, and for repayments of CGT if the earn-out is never actually paid.

  If the deferred payments are uncertain at the time the company is sold – such as "40% of the profits made by the company in the next two years" – the treatment is different.

  The right to these future payments has to be valued at the time of the sale, and this value is taxed as part of the sale proceeds.

  When and if the earn out payments are made, the vendor is taxed on the difference between the value ascribed to the earn out, and the amount received.

Case Study - 37 Taxation of Uncertain Earn-Out

Sam sells his trading company for £200,000 cash upfront, and 40% of the profits of the company in the year after the sale, payable four months after the end of that year when the accounts are signed off.

For the last three years the company's profits have averaged £250,000, so if all goes well, Sam expects to receive £100,000 for the earn-out. The cost of Sam's shares was a nominal £1, as he started the company himself from scratch three years ago.

It is agreed with HMRC that at the time of the sale, the value of the right to 40% of next year's profits, payable in 16 months' time, is £60,000. (This valuation takes account of both the fact that the amount of the payment is uncertain, and that Sam will have to wait for his money).

On the sale of the company, Sam's CGT computation looks like this:

Sale cash	200,000
Value of earn-out	60,000
Total gain	260,000

Taxable gain	65,000

16 months later, it turns out that the company's profits were £200,000 for the year, so Sam's earn-out payment is £80,000.

His tax computation looks like this:

Payment received	80,000
Less value of earn-out	(65,000)
Taxable gain	15,000

Note that Sam gets no taper relief on his earn-out – it is not a business asset, and he has owned it for less than three years.

There are ways around the taper relief problem here, involving the issue of shares or a special type of "loan note" instead of cash, but this is sophisticated tax planning and expert advice is essential.

15.4.2. "Employment-Related Shares or Securities"

If the vendor is required to stay on as a director of the company for the earn-out period, as often happens so that he can "hand over the reins" to the new owners (and make sure his earn-out is as big as possible!), great care needs to be taken to make sure that he does not fall foul of the rules on "employment related securities" – see Case Study - 32.

If the earn-out is paid in the form of loan notes or shares (perhaps to get round the taper relief problem in Case Study - 37) there is a danger that these will be treated as chargeable to income tax (on their market value) rather than to CGT – again, there are ways round this, with good tax advice on the specific circumstances

15.4.3. Payments Under Warranties and Indemnities

The vendor often has to agree to pay the purchaser some sort of compensation if the company turns out not to be worth as much as he was told, or if there are unexpected tax liabilities.

It is important that the Sale Agreement is so worded that these are treated as refunds of the purchase price so that the vendor can get a CGT repayment, and the purchaser is not taxed on the payment until he eventually sells the shares.

15.4.4. *"Compensation for Loss of Office"*

There is an exemption from income tax and NIC for up to £30,000 paid to an employee who is sacked or made redundant, and Sale Agreements for companies quite often include provisions for £30,000 to be paid to the vendor (who will of course be expected to resign from his directorship when he sells his shares).

Most of these "compensation payments" do not come within the exemption, and can cause tax problems for both the vendor and the company (which will then go for compensation from the vendor under the warranties and indemnities).

In some circumstances, these payments can be made tax free, but again this is an area for expert advice.

15.4.5. *Pre-Sale Tax Planning*

This ranges from simple things like getting cash out of the company before the sale (as most vendors are not prepared to "buy" cash in a company's bank account), through more sophisticated ideas like the ones mentioned above concerning earn-outs, to positively heroic enterprises such as moving to a tax haven for five years to escape CGT entirely (and yes, it has to be for five complete tax years).

15.4.6. *Company Purchase of Own Shares*

In some cases, rather than sell the shares to the purchaser directly, it may be possible for the company itself to buy them back from the vendor.

Case Study - 38 Company Purchase of Own Shares

Bill and Ben own 50% each of the shares in a trading company. Bill is older than Ben, and wants to retire. Bill and Ben agree that Bill's shares are worth £200,000, but Ben cannot afford to buy him out.

The company has £100,000 cash, however, and can easily raise another £100,000 on the security of its factory, which is owned by the company.

Bill's Tax Adviser explains that provided certain conditions are fulfilled, and a "clearance" is obtained from HMRC, it will be possible for the company to buy Bill's shares from him, and for the sale to be treated as giving rise to a capital gain – (normally, if a company buys shares back from its shareholders, this is treated as if the company has paid them a dividend).

The "clearance" is obtained, and the company buys Bill's shares for £200,000. Bill pays CGT on his gain (reduced by 75% because of business taper relief).

The effect of the company buying these shares is that they cease to exist, and so Ben is now the sole owner of the company.

This special treatment is only available to a company that is trading. If the shares in a property investment company are bought back, this will be treated as if the company had paid a dividend – but this is not always a bad thing:

Case Study - 39 Purchase of Own Shares Treated as a Distribution

Purchase of own shares treated as a distribution.

The facts are as in Case Study 38, except that the company is a recently formed property investment company. Bill, who wants to retire, has a very low base cost (£1) for his shares, and as he has only owned them for two years, he would get no taper relief on the shares at all. He would therefore pay CGT at 40% on a gain of £200,000 = £80,000.

If instead the company buys his shares, he will be taxed as if it had paid him a dividend, so he will pay tax at 25% on the £200,000 = £50,000. Even if Ben could have afforded to buy his shares, by selling them to the company, he has saved tax of £30,000.

15.4.7. Timing

Capital gains tax is payable on 31 January after the end of the year of assessment in which the gain is made, so for a sale on 5 April 2006 (i.e., in 2005/06), the tax is due on 31 January 2007.

For a sale on 6 April 2006 (i.e., in 2006/07) the tax is payable a whole year later, on 31 January 2008.

Bear in mind that for CGT a sale takes place on the date the contract is signed, not, if later, the day the asset is transferred to the new owner, so simply exchanging contracts on 5 April with completion at a later date will not push the sale into the next tax year.

"Options" can be used to try to "lock in" the deal but delay it to the next tax year, but beware – unless carefully done, these can prevent taper relief being available during the period of the option.

(An "option" is simply an agreement between A and B that A will sell an asset to B at a future date – a "call" option, or that B will buy the asset from A – a "put" option).

15.4.8. Gifts to Spouse

In some circumstances, it makes sense to make a gift of some of your shares to your spouse before a sale, to use their annual exemption and their lower rates of tax, if any, but there are pitfalls:

- **Taper relief.** If the asset in question is shares, you can sometimes lose business asset taper relief if you gift the shares to your spouse. Check with your tax adviser before making the gift.

- **"Imperfect" gifts.** Make sure you actually do make the gift, and that you do it before the sale has been agreed, and that the spouse is included in the Sale Agreement (it is surprising how often this last point is forgotten).

  HMRC are becoming particularly "hot" on this point – if the gift is not properly evidenced – for example if the share transfer document is not sent to Companies House – or if the sale has already been agreed when the gift is made, HMRC will argue that all that was given was a proportion of the sale proceeds, and not the shares themselves.

Case Study - 40 Pre-Sale Gift to Spouse

Gordon is negotiating to sell his company, of which he has owned all the 100 shares for five years, for £300,000. The base cost of his shares is only £100. He pays tax at 40%.

The company is a property investment company, so he does not have to worry about business taper relief problems, and he gifts 20 shares to his wife, who has no income or gains for the year of the sale. He does this before he has reached any agreements to sell the company – in fact there are three possible purchasers competing with each other for it. There is no CGT on gifts between husband and wife.

The company sells for £310,000, which is £3,100 for each of the 100 shares. Gordon's wife pays CGT on her shares like this;

Gain on sale (20 x 3,100)	62,000
Taper relief (15%)	(9,300)
Gain	52,700
Annual exemption	(9,200)
Taxable	43,500
Tax on first 2,230 at 10%	223
Tax on next 32,370 at 20%	6,474
Tax on remaining 8,900 at 40%	3,560
Total tax	10,257
Saving compared to 40% on 52,700	10,823

Gordon's wife's annual exemption and lower rate bands have saved tax of £10,823 compared to the 40% tax Gordon would have paid.

15.4.9. Substantial Shareholding Exemption

This only applies when a company sells its shares in another company, not when an individual sells shares.

In certain (complicated) circumstances, a company is exempt from tax on a capital gain it makes when it sells shares in another company which it owns.

The details of this relief are very complex, but if a trading company has owned more than 10% of the shares in another trading company for at least a year, and it then sells those shares, it may qualify for the exemption and not have to pay corporation tax on any gain it makes on those shares.

Of course, from the point of view of the shareholders in the vendor company, they still have to find a way to get the cash out of the company.

15.4.10. Post Sale Tax Planning

There is much less scope for this than there is for pre-sale tax planning, which is why it is important to take tax advice **before** a sale.

15.4.11. Tax Shelters

This does not refer to "tax haven" countries, but to approved investments that offer tax deferral, such as the EIS – see section 10.2.1.

15.4.12. Losses

Losses on investments in the same or previous tax year can be set against gains of the same tax year, so now might be the time to sell off assets that will produce a loss – but if you are getting business taper relief on your capital gain, think twice, because losses are deducted BEFORE taper relief.

Case Study - 41 Taper Relief and Losses

Dominic is selling his trading company and makes a gain of £100,000 before taper relief. He also has some other investments which will realise a loss for CGT if he sells them, of £10,000.

He rushes to sell them in the same tax year as the sale of the shares, so he can deduct the loss from the gain. In the following tax year, he sells an investment property (which he has only owned for 2 years, so no taper relief), making another gain of £100,000.

In year 1, his gains are:

Gain before taper	100,000
Less losses	(10,000)
Gain	90,000
Business taper relief 75%	(67,500)
Taxable gain	22,500

In year 2, the position is:

Gain before taper	100,000
Less losses	NIL
Gain	100,000
taper relief	NIL
Taxable gain	100,000

If Gordon had delayed selling the loss-making assets until after the end of the first tax year, the position would have been:

In Year 1:

Gain before taper	100,000
Less losses	Nil
Gain	100,000
Business taper relief 75%	(75,000)
Taxable gain	25,000

In Year 2:

Gain before taper	100,000
Less losses	(10,000)
Gain	90,000
taper relief	NIL
Taxable gain	90,000

Because he set the losses against the business taper gain, the losses themselves were effectively tapered, and so the 10,000 loss only reduced the gain by 2,500, whereas by deferring the loss until the next tax year, it was worth the full £10,000 – a difference of £7,500.

15.5. Sales of Assets and Liquidation of Company

Although it is seldom the most tax efficient way to dispose of a company, this route is often forced on the vendor because the purchaser refuses to buy the shares instead, for the reasons already explained earlier in this section.

Once the assets of the business have been sold by the company, and it has paid the resulting corporation tax on its gains, we are left with what is sometimes known as a "cash-box" company – that is, a company whose only asset is a large bank balance. Unless the company plans to use this cash to start a new business venture, of course, the question is how to get the cash out.

What happens next?

If the company pays the cash out to its shareholders as a dividend, they will suffer income tax at 25% on that dividend (assuming they are higher rate taxpayers).

The alternative is to wind up the company and distribute its assets to its members.

This will be treated as a disposal of their shares for CGT purposes, and so they will pay CGT based on the cost of their shares, and how long they have owned them.

Golden Rule

Do not assume that liquidation will always be better than a dividend.

15.6. Dividend versus Liquidation

Consider the following case study:

Case Study - 42 Dividend Versus Liquidation

Propco Ltd is a property investment company, set up two years ago by Steve, who is the sole shareholder. His 100 shares cost him £100. He pays income tax at 40% as he has a well paid job. He is married to Jane, who has no income.

After selling all its properties and paying all its tax, Propco is left with £700,000 in the bank, and no other assets or liabilities. Steve and Jane decide to get the cash out of the company.

Assuming in either case that Steve gives half his shares to Jane before anything else is done, we need to compare the tax effect of the company paying a dividend of £350,000 to each of them, or of liquidating the company and paying CGT on a gain of £350,000 each.

Looking at a dividend first, then at liquidation:

	Steve	**Jane**	**Total**
Dividend income	350,000	350,000	700,000
Less personal allowance	Used elsewhere	(5,225)	(5,225)
Tax on first 34,600	N/A	NIL	NIL
Tax on balance	87,500	78, 539	166,039
Liquidation gain (no taper)	350,000	350,000	700,000
Annual exemption	(9,200)	(9,200)	(18,400)
CGT at 10%	NIL	223	223
CGT at 20%	NIL	6,474	6,474
CGT at 40%	136,320	122,480	258,800
Tax saving through dividend	48,820	50,638	99,458

It would have been all too easy to rush into a liquidation that would have cost them over £90,000 in tax. Notice also that the saving does not entirely depend on using Jane's lower rates and exemptions – Steve, who pays higher rate tax on all his gains and income, saves £48,820 by taking a dividend.

Essentially, it all depends on the rate of CGT that the shareholders will pay on their gains if the company is liquidated.

In some cases, a combination of a dividend first, and then a liquidation, will produce the best result.

15.7. How to Liquidate a Company

There are two ways a company can be liquidated – the formal and the informal way.

15.7.1. A Formal Liquidation

A formal liquidation must be done by a specialised accountant called a "licensed insolvency practitioner".

It tends to be expensive (not least because in some circumstances a licensed insolvency practitioner can become personally liable to the company's creditors if he gets things wrong!), but it is sometimes necessary due to the nature of the company's business – ask your accountant to advise you.

15.7.2. An Informal Liquidation

This form of liquidation is also known as **"striking-off", or "an ESC C16".** This is by far the commonest form of liquidation, and it goes like this:

- The company pays all its debts and collects everything owed to it.

- It then approaches the inspector of taxes and asks him to confirm that **Extra Statutory Concession C 16** will apply – without this assurance, when the company pays out its cash, this would be treated as a dividend for tax purposes, but under ESC C16 HMRC agree to treat it as giving rise to a capital gain as with a formal liquidation.

- Having got the inspector's confirmation that ESC C16 will be applied, the company pays out all its cash to its shareholders (it is also possible for the company to transfer any assets it may have such as a property, though this is a little more complicated to arrange). The shareholders are treated as if they had sold their shares for the amount of cash or other assets they receive.

- Finally, the company applies to the Registrar of Companies to be "struck off" the Register of Companies. Once the Registrar has done this the company is dead – though, like Dracula, it can sometimes be revived if unforseen liabilities appear.

15.8. Dying in Harness

Many businessmen take the view that their company is their pension, and as such, they have no plans to liquidate or sell. Instead, the company will pay them dividends which they will live on in their retirement.

This may be a reasonable strategy, but it is important to take account of another tax we have not yet looked at – inheritance tax.

Perhaps appropriately, the final chapter of this guide deals with this.

16. Inheritance Tax and Companies

Most explanations of inheritance tax ("IHT") begin with a weak joke about "death and taxes", but it is important to realise that IHT is not only a tax on death. In a number of situations, it can be payable during your lifetime.

This guide is not the place for a detailed study of all the IHT planning techniques, but in this chapter, I want to look at some examples of how IHT interacts with property companies.

16.1. IHT – the basics

IHT is charged on "transfers of value". The commonest "transfer of value" is a gift, but as we shall see, there are other things which, sometimes unexpectedly, are transfers of value.

When a person dies, they are charged to IHT as if they had made a transfer of value of everything they owned on the day they died. In addition, any transfers of value they made in the seven years ending on the date they died are also included.

IHT is charged at the following rates, depending on whether the transfer of value was made during a person's lifetime, or on his death:

Transfer of value	Death Rate	Lifetime Rate
0 – 300,000	0%	0%
Above 300,000	40%	20%

Golden Rule

The first £300,000, which is charged at 0%, is called the nil rate band ("NRB"). It is often referred to as an "exemption", but this is a misleading way to think about it, as we shall see.

16.2. PETs

Not all transfers of value attract IHT when they are made. A simple gift from one individual to another will be a "potentially exempt transfer" ("PET").

This means that if the individual making the gift lives for another seven years after making it, it will fall out of account and no IHT will be charged on it when the individual dies. If, however, they die within seven years, it will form part of their estate at death.

Case Study - 43 A Failed PET

Joe is a middle aged widower. On 1 April 2006, he makes a cash gift to his son of £100,000, to help him buy a house. This is a PET for IHT purposes, and so there is no IHT to pay at the time. Sadly, during 2007, Joe is killed in a car crash. His estate at death, after deducting all debts, is worth £250,000.

Because Joe has not survived for seven years after making the gift to his son, the PET is added to his estate when calculating the IHT:

Value of estate at death	250,000
Add gifts in last seven years	100,000
Total	350,000
Deduct NRB	(300,000)
Chargeable to IHT at 40%	50,000

16.3. Gift With Reservation of Benefit

A gift is only a PET if it is really given away. If the person making the gift continues to enjoy a benefit from it, it will be a **"gift with reservation of benefit. ("GWROB").** It will still be treated as owned by the giver. The commonest example of a GWROB is where a parent gifts their house to their child, but continues to live there, but any gift which the giver continues to enjoy will be a GWROB:

Case Study - 44 GWROB

Sue is a widow, getting on in years, and like many otherwise modestly off people, she has one hugely valuable asset – her house. It is worth £350,000, and the mortgage was paid off long ago. The rest of her assets come to £200,000.

She makes a gift of the house to her two children, but continues to live in it. 10 years later she dies, still living in the house.

Because she "reserved a benefit" in the house, by continuing to live in it, for IHT purposes she is treated as if she still owned the house, so the value of her death estate is £550,000. It is irrelevant that she has survived for over seven years since she gave the house away – for IHT purposes it is still hers.

16.4. Spouse Exemption

A gift or a legacy from one spouse to the other is exempt from IHT. If you die and leave everything absolutely to your spouse, there will be no IHT to pay.

16.5. Business Property Relief

For IHT purposes, "business property" gets relief at either 50% or 100%, depending on its nature. The crucial types of business property for property investors are:

- An interest in a business (that is, a sole trader, or a partner)
- Shares in an unlisted trading company

Both these can qualify for 100% BPR, and thus effectively be exempt from IHT, but it is crucial to remember that a "business" or a "trading company" does **NOT** include a business that involves:

- Making or holding investments – and HMRC regard property letting as falling into this category
- Dealing in land – although a property development company **may** qualify as long as it is really "developing" property – new builds or major refurbishments – and not simply buying and selling properties

Most property companies, therefore, are unlikely to qualify for Business Property Relief, and so the planning for them will tend to involve making gifts during the owner's lifetime, and hoping to survive the necessary seven years.

This guide is not the place to look at the various planning strategies to minimise IHT – this is a huge subject, and there is probably no area of taxation where skilled professional advice is more ESSENTIAL to avoid pitfalls.

Caution

It is not an exaggeration to say that any layman who attempts to do any IHT planning more sophisticated than leaving everything to his wife is likely to produce unexpected and expensive results for himself and his family.

Even leaving everything to your wife could be a mistake.

16.6. Close Companies and IHT

IHT is essentially a tax on individuals (and Trusts), and there is a common misconception that it cannot apply to companies. This is generally the case, but there are exceptions:

Case Study - 45 Transfer of Value by a Close Company

Mr Smart is a widower and the sole owner of a property investment company. The value of his 100 £1 shares is £1million. Mindful of the IHT consequences if he dies still owning all of it (no BPR, so fully chargeable to IHT), he wants to give half the company to his son (who is not involved with the company, having a full time job of his own).

He knows that if he simply gifts 50 shares to his son, he will be treated as having sold them for market value and will pay CGT on £500,000, so he comes up with another idea – he gets his son to subscribe for 100 new shares, paying their face value of £1 each.

Unfortunately, this is one of those rare examples where a close company can be involved in a transfer of value for IHT.

Because his son paid much less than market value for the shares, the shareholders before the shares were issued (here, Mr Smart) are treated as having made a transfer of value for IHT – and this type of transfer is not a gift from one individual to another, so it cannot be a PET.

It is immediately chargeable to IHT at the lifetime rate of 20%.

The amount of the transfer is the amount by which Mr Smart's estate has reduced in value, not the amount received by his son, so it is not £499,900 (the difference between the value of the shares and the amount he paid the company for them). Instead, we look at Mr Smart:

The value of each share before the issue to his son was £10,000 (1,000,000 divided by 100).

After the share issue, Mr Smart no longer has absolute control of the company, because he only has half the shares and cannot outvote his son if there is a dispute.

It is normal to discount the value of the shares by around 20% (it would have been more for a trading company) to reflect the fact that the shareholder has less than absolute control over the underlying assets in the company.

The value of Mr Smart's 100 shares is therefore £500,000 (half the value of the whole company), less £100,000 (20% discount for loss of control of company), so his shares are now worth £400,000. His transfer of value is therefore:

Value of 100 shares before share issue	1,000,000
Less value of 100 shares after share issue	(400,000)

Deemed transfer of value	600,000
Less NRB	(300,000)
Chargeable to IHT at 20%	300,000
IHT payable	60,000

Note – because of the way IHT is calculated on transfers like this, the actual amount might be somewhat different, but for simplicity, £60,000 gives a good idea of the amount due.

It does not end there – there is anti avoidance legislation for CGT, which means that Mr Smart is treated as having made a disposal for CGT purposes of £500,000, by "value shifting".

Fortunately for him, however, because the transfer was immediately chargeable to IHT, he can "hold over" this gain, in much the same way as he could have done if the shares had been shares in a trading company.

The above example was a disaster for Mr Smart, because he did not realise the IHT he would have to pay, but in fact much IHT planning for property investment companies revolves around deliberately incurring IHT charges (but usually, carefully kept within the £300,000 nil rate band so as not to have to actually pay any IHT) as a way of holding over the capital gain on a gift of the shares.

I do not propose to go into detail on IHT planning for property companies – it really is a case of "don't try this at home" – but I hope you will realise from the above that IHT cannot be ignored by owners of property companies, even though they may not be around when the time comes to pay the tax!

To end on a piece of good news – IHT is normally payable (broadly) nine months after the transfer of value (or the date of death), but where it is charged on property deriving its value from land, it is often possible to arrange to pay the tax in ten annual instalments – the idea being, that the property need not be sold off to pay the IHT.

Good Advisors do Save You TAX!

17. Finding an Accountant

There is a saying, "a good accountant pays for him/herself". Never a truer word has been spoken.

In this chapter we will become familiar with and understand how to acquire the services of an excellent accountant.

17.1. Accountants Qualifications

The first step is to ensure that your accountant is a member of a recognised institute.

Some of the popular ones amongst accountants are ACA, ACCA, ICAEW, ICAS etc.

Here is what these abbreviations stand for:

- Association of Chartered Accountants (ACA)
- Association of Chartered Certified Accountants (ACCA)
- Institute of Chartered Accountants in England and Wales (ICAEW)
- Institute of Chartered Accountants in Scotland (ICAS)

Furthermore it would not be a bad idea to pick an accountant who is a member of the Chartered Institute of Taxation or Association of Taxation Technicians.

Getting to know the history of your proposed accountant is a very good idea, so look for the following signs:

a) Are they a former Tax Inspector?
b) Have they passed the Taxation (ATII, ATT) exams?

A qualified tax advisor is useful for all sorts of tax related services and these include:

- Preparing tax returns
- Sole trader tax returns
- Tax planning advice

It is most likely that your tax advisor will charge on an hourly basis. However some will agree a flat fee beforehand.

It is pertinent to ask whether one should go for a general or specialist tax advisor, although it may seem better to go with the general advisor as he/she will most definitely be cheaper.

However in the long-term the specialist may save you money because of his/her in depth knowledge and experience.

17.2. General Advisor or Tax Specialist?

A specialist will have the answer, usually to hand, whereas a non specialist may have to consult HMRC documentation or may indeed consult the specialist and then pass the charge back on to you.

Cost can be a significant issue as a specialist can charge around £270 per hour. For this you get about 15 minutes of quizzing followed by 45 minutes worth of (in most cases) written response (Oh and that's plus VAT!)

To put that into perspective a non specialist can charge around £150 per hour. A typical session with a non specialist can take up to 2.5 hours. This time would be typically spent in the following way:

- 15 minutes of clarification.
- 1.5 hours of research.
- 45 minutes of written response.

As you can see sometimes it is beneficial if you go direct to a specialist, particularly if your questions to your accountant require him/her to study before responding.

With the above two examples in mind it is important to ascertain a working relationship with your advisor. You should be familiar with his/her area of expertise and know what their limitations are i.e. what they are not too hot on.

17.3. How to Choose Your Adviser

Before you sign up with a tax adviser or accountant, be sure to address the following:

17.3.1. Will I Need a Tax Adviser or an Accountant?

More often that not people will actually require both, however, it is important to establish why you need them- do you need someone to manage your accounts and help you with your tax return, or someone to give you sound advice that will legally save you money. Your accountant can manage your accounts, provide compliance work and some may even do tax planning.

However, tax advisers tend to focus solely on tax planning. They spend significant amounts of time keeping up-to-date with the latest tax legislation and tax cases to help make sure they provide their clients with great strategies that will help to reduce or eliminate tax - some of which your accountant may not even be aware of!

If we compare the accountancy profession with medicine, an accountant is the equivalent of a GP, and most of the time a GP is all you need for routine health care, but if you get seriously ill (compare with a dispute with HM Revenue and Customs) or you need surgery (tax planning), then you need a specialist consultant (a Tax Adviser).

17.3.2. What Qualifications?

As a client you want to be assured that your tax adviser / accountant is acting in both your best interest and within the law, which is why it is important to know what qualifications your tax adviser or accountant has, and when they were achieved and if they are relevant to you. Check that the qualifications they have cover the area of taxation or accounting that you require assistance with.

17.3.3. How Much Experience do they Have?

When choosing a tax adviser or accountant, it is good to know just how much experience they have and what their reputation is.

Do not be afraid to ask how long have they been giving advice, where they worked before or if they have ever done any public speaking or written work that you can refer back to? Another good question to ask is how many existing clients they have within the area that you are interested in, for example – if you develop property, how many other developers have they provided advice for and will they be able to provide references?

Good advisers will boast about their success, so give them to the opportunity to do so!

17.3.4. How Much Will it Cost?

That really does depend on what type of advice or service you require. The fees generally reflect the adviser's / accountant's level of experience and qualifications, along with the amount of time they may have to spend on your case; in this instance you can request an estimate of the total. Also ask when fees need to be paid by.

Some accountants and tax advisers do offer 'fixed fees' for certain types of advice or help so that you know exactly what you are paying and exactly what you will receive.

Try to negotiate a fixed fee wherever possible, as good advisers won't be afraid to operate on this basis. It is far better than the 'let the clock run' approach, though in some cases such as a tax investigation, hourly charges are the only practical way to work.

17.3.5. Professional Bodies

There are various professional bodies that you will find tax advisers and accountants to be part of.

Anybody who claims to be able to give 'tax advice' should be a 'Chartered Tax Adviser' (CTA), which means that they will be member of the Chartered Institute of Taxation and will have taken and passed their examinations.

Qualified accountants will have Chartered Certified Accountant (ACCA or FCCA), or Chartered Accountant (CA, ACA or FCA) in their title.

17.3.6. What About Indemnity Cover?

If an adviser gives you inappropriate advice or your accountant does not manage your accounts correctly it could result in a huge financial loss for you.

Finding out at the beginning what indemnity cover a tax adviser or accountant has will mean peace of mind for you. Find out whether they are covered for loss of documents, court attendance and legal fees, breach of confidence or misuse of information to suggest just a few areas. Ask who they are covered by and for how much per claim.

Knowing what protection your adviser or accountant has will protect you. You will be alarmed to learn that some advisers do not even have indemnity cover and you are well advised to stay away from such advisers. Chartered accountants and Chartered Tax Advisers are required by the rules of their professional bodies to have professional indemnity insurance.

17.3.7. How do I Contact My Tax Adviser / Accountant?

It can be quite frustrating when each time you phone your tax adviser or accountant they are unavailable.

Find out in advance how to contact them and if this suits you. If you are whether that the procedure is to leave a message with the secretary, that you will be dealing directly with the adviser, or that you will be put through to another adviser you will feel more comfortable.

If you have 'ad-hoc' questions to ask your adviser or accountant and you cannot reach them, how soon will they get back to you? Also, find out if they are happy to receive email as you may prefer this method of correspondence.

Your chosen advisers should personally respond to your enquiries and calls within an agreed timescale.

A recent development has been the growth of online accountants and tax advisers, and if you do not feel the need for face to face contact with your adviser, you may want to consider using such a firm. Having lower overheads in the form of offices and meeting rooms, they are often able to offer lower fees than the conventional firms.

17.3.8. Keep up to Date with Tax Legislation Changes

Tax legislation is constantly changing. That is why it is important that your adviser or accountant keeps up-to-date with all the changes.

Also, to retain their qualifications, tax advisers and accountants must adhere to ongoing training programmes enforced by their regulatory bodies, to ensure that they are keeping abreast of the latest changes in legislation and the latest tax planning opportunities.

For Example, CPD (Continuing Professional Development) is the compulsory training a Chartered Tax Adviser is required to do each year in order to keep his qualifications. He or she must do a minimum of 90 hours training per year; broken down into at least 20 hours "structured" training - that is, attending seminars, lectures, etc, and 70 hours "unstructured" training (such as reading textbooks and technical articles)

17.3.9. What if I Have an Emergency?

You are now aware of how to contact your tax adviser or accountant but what happens if you have an emergency and need urgent tax advice?

How available are they in a crisis?

Knowing that you can rely on the tax adviser or accountant is an important point when considering their services. Make sure that you are able to contact them without having to arrange a formal meeting!

17.3.10. Does the Adviser Sell 'off the Shelf' Packages?

This is a very important question to ask your adviser. There are certain advisers out there who sell tax schemes (also known as 'off the shelf' tax solutions) and earn significant amounts of commission by doing so.

"Tax Schemes" come in all sorts of forms – one example (attacked by some legislation announced in the Pre-Budget Report) is the creation of artificial capital losses to set against capital gains.

If you adviser mentions such schemes to you, then be cautious as HM Revenue and Customs are getting tough on such schemes, and legislation has been introduced requiring those using them to disclose the fact to HMRC.

18. The Importance of Tax Planning

We all instinctively do some tax planning in our daily lives, even if it is simply remembering to buy our "duty frees" when we return from our holiday abroad.

If you are going to make the best of your property business, then you need to be alert to the tax implications of your business plans, and to any opportunities to reduce the likely tax bill. Your instinct may be enough for your duty free goodies, but for tax on your business, you need a more structured approach!

"Tax planning" means arranging your business affairs so that you pay the minimum amount of tax that the law requires. It does not mean trying to conceal things from the Taxman, and it does not mean indulging in highly complex (and expensive!) artificial "tax avoidance" schemes.

"Every man is entitled if he can to order his affairs so that the tax attaching under the appropriate Acts is less than it would otherwise be." That is what the House of Lords said in 1935, when they found for the Duke of Westminster and against the Inland Revenue. This still holds true today, though there is now a mass of "anti-avoidance" legislation to consider when thinking about tax planning – and before you ask, the Duke's tax planning idea was stopped by anti-avoidance legislation!

18.1. Knowing When to Consider Planning

A question you will most certainly ask yourself is 'when should I consider tax planning for my property business?'

The short answer is "all the time", but to be realistic, no-one is likely to do this. The trick is to develop by experience, a sense of when a tax planning opportunity (or a potentially expensive tax pitfall) is likely to present itself.

You should consider tax planning in all of the following situations, for example:

18.1.1. Buying

If you are buying a property, you need to consider:

- Buying the property – It could be you as an individual, you and your spouse, you and a business partner, a Limited Company owned by you, or perhaps a Trust you have set up. Your decision will depend on your future business strategy

- Financing the property – You will need to consider whether you are taking out a mortgage, and if so how will it be secured. It may not always make sense to secure the loan on the property you are buying if you have other assets on which you can secure the loan.

- Plans for the property – It could be that you are you buying the property to sell it again in the short term, or to hold it long term and benefit from the rental income. The tax treatment will be different according to which is the case, and different planning should be done before the property is bought.

18.1.2. Repairs and Refurbishment

If you spend money on a property, you need to consider:

- Whether you doing it in order to sell it again in the short term, or whether you will continue letting it.

- If the work being done is classed as a **repair** to the property, or an **improvement.** See icon below for the difference between the two.

The distinction between a repair and an improvement to a property is very important, because although the cost of repairs can be deducted from your rental income for tax purposes, an improvement can only be claimed as a deduction against CGT when you sell the property.

Essentially, a repair is when you replace like with like, whereas an improvement involves adding to the property (say, a conservatory or a loft conversion), or replacing something with something significantly better (say, removing the old storage heaters and installing oil-fired central heating).

HMRC do not always behave logically when it comes to repairs versus improvements.

A client of mine sold a seaside property, in circumstances where he would have to pay CGT on the sale profit. He had spent a lot of money on this property, which when he bought it had not been touched since the early 1950s.

He had ripped out the old "utility" kitchen, for example, and replaced it with a state-of –the –art designer affair in gleaming slate, chrome, and steel. The old 1950s cooker had had some bakelite knobs to turn the gas on and off – the new kitchen range had the computer power of the average 1970s space capsule.

Clearly an improvement, and so deductible from his capital gain, but HMRC tried to argue that one kitchen is much like another and he was just replacing like with like – so they said it was a repair, which was no good to him in his case as there was no rental income from which he could deduct the cost of repairs.

18.1.3. Selling

When you decide to dispose of a property, there are other tax issues to consider:

- Who is the property going to? – If it is to someone "connected" with you, such as a close relative or a business partner, and if you do not charge them the full market value, HMRC can step in and tax you as if you had sold it for full value.

- Will you be paying CGT or income tax on the profit you make? – The planning opportunities are very different, depending on which tax is involved.

- What are the terms of the sale? Is it just a cash sale, or is the buyer a developer who is offering you a "slice of the action" in the form of a share of the profits from the development? There is important anti-avoidance legislation to consider if this is the case.

18.1.4. Life changes

Whenever your life undergoes some significant changes, you should consider tax planning.

Here are some examples when tax planning should be considered:

- Getting married – a married couple (and a civil partnership) have a number of tax planning opportunities denied to single people, but there are also one or two pitfalls to watch out for.

- Moving house – it is usually not a good idea to sell the old house immediately, as there are often tax advantages to keeping it and letting it out.

- Changing your job. You may become a higher or lower rate tax payer and this may mean you should change your tax strategy.

  If you are moving house, and you sell the old residence, you will have the cash left after you have paid off the mortgage and the various removal costs to spend on your new home. If you need a mortgage to buy the new home, the interest on that mortgage is not allowed as a deduction for tax purposes.

  If, instead, you remortgage the old house and let it out, ALL the mortgage interest you pay can be deducted against the rent you receive whatever you do with the cash you have released – and you may well be able to sell the house after three years of letting (or sometimes a longer period), and pay no CGT on the increased value since you stopped living there.

- Death – IHT is charged at 40% on the value of your estate when you die, to the extent that the value is greater than (for 2007/08) £300,000. By planning early enough it is possible to reduce the IHT burden considerably.

18.1.5. Politics

There are two occasions each year when you need to be particularly alert – the Pre Budget Report in November or December, and The Budget in March.

On both these occasions the Chancellor of the Exchequer announces tax rates, and new tax legislation, which might well affect you and your property business. In some cases, however, new tax legislation is announced at other times – it pays to keep a weather eye on the financial pages of the newspaper, or to subscribe to a magazine or journal that will alert you to important tax changes that may affect your business.

18.1.6. *End and Start of Tax Year*

The tax year ends on the 5th April each year and it is a good idea to review your tax situation before this date to make sure you are not missing any planning opportunities.

18.2. The Real Benefits of Tax Planning

Robert Kiyosaki, author of the number one bestselling book 'Rich Dad Poor Dad', says '*Every time people try to punish the rich, the rich don't simply comply, they react. They have the money, power and intent to change things. They do not sit there and voluntarily pay more taxes. They search for ways to minimize their tax burden'*
The whole purpose of tax planning is to save you tax and to put more profits in your pocket. That is why the rich are always looking at ways of beating the taxman, because they benefits of tax planning.

18.2.1. *Paying Less Tax*

Don't fall into the trap where you only think about tax when you are considering selling or even worse after you have sold the property.

By taking tax advice at the right times and on a regular basis you will legitimately avoid or reduce taxes both in the short and the long term.

This means that you will have greater profits to spend as you wish.

18.2.2. *Clear 'Entrance' and 'Exit' Strategies*

When you sit down and analyse properties that you are considering for investment, you will no doubt look at how much rental income the property will generate and what you expect to achieve in capital appreciation.

Knowing the estimated tax liabilities right from the outset will save you from any nasty surprises in the future.

> Your personal circumstances can change at a whim. The last thing that you want to do is fall into a situation where you are forced to sell a property but are unable to pay the taxman because you never considered your tax situation.

18.2.3. *Staying Focused*

When you are deciding on the property investment strategies that you are going to adopt it is a good idea to talk them through with a tax adviser.

If your investment strategy changes then it is likely to have an impact on your tax strategy so it should be reviewed with your tax adviser.

Your tax strategy will go hand in hand with your investment strategy and will help you to keep focused on your property investment and financial goals.

18.2.4. Improving Cash Flow

One of the challenges that you will face as a property investor is cash flow. In other words, you need to make sure that you have enough money coming in from your property business to pay for all property related bills, maintenance and repairs, and of course tax on the rental profits.

Remember, timing of expenditures can be the difference between a 'high' and a 'nil' tax bill. Therefore, keeping in regular contact with your tax adviser, especially when coming towards the end of the tax year can have a significant impact on your property cash flow.

18.2.5. Avoiding Common Tax Traps

There are many tax traps that you can fall into if you have not taken any tax advice at all, not to mention the numerous great tax planning opportunities you will miss out on too.

In is not uncommon to hear stories about investors who have made a £100,000 profit on a single property and then sold it without taking any tax advice whatsoever. If you fall into this situation then you could be facing a tax bill of up to £40,000.

It will hurt you even more if after selling you realise that you could have easily turned the tax liability to zero had you taken some simple tax advice.

Good tax advisers will know of the most common traps that you are likely to fall into, so a few minutes spent wisely could save you thousands in taxes.

18.3. The Golden Tax Rules

The challenge to you as a property investor will no doubt be how to grow a profitable portfolio. One of the easiest ways you can make money in property is to pay less tax.

18.3.1. Education...Education...Education

Whether you are starting out in property investing or are an experienced landlord with a sizeable portfolio, there is one thing that you should always do - educate yourself to make sure you are:

a) complying with the ever changing legal requirements

b) learning how to make your investments more profitable

c) making sure you keep up-to-date with tax changes that may affect your tax liability.

Although there is never a substitute for taking professional advice, you should keep yourself updated so that you can discuss these opportunities with your adviser at your next appointment.

18.3.2. Prevention is Better Than Cure

There is a proverb 'prevention is better than cure' (believe it or not this was first said by the famous medieval philosopher Erasmus) and he probably was not thinking about tax when he said it, but it most certainly applies.

Planning for a tax situation you are likely to face is much better than trying to get out of a tax problem that you have unknowingly (or even knowingly) fallen into. It is certain that trying to get out of a tax problem will cost much more in specialist/consultancy fees and there is never a guarantee that you will get out of the problem.

Congratulations – You've now finished 'How to Use Companies to Slash Your Property Taxes'

To learn even more ways on how to legitimately cut your property tax bills please visit: www.property-tax-portal.co.uk.

Special Bonus Report

Companies and Overseas Property Investment

By Daniel Feingold

19. International and Offshore Companies by Daniel Feingold

So far in this guide we have looked at UK companies for UK property investments.

However, a growing number of people are now investing overseas. Whenever this happens investors are never sure which type of structure to use for such investments.

In this chapter International and offshore tax specialist, Daniel Feingold, goes through the different options that are available.

19.1. About Daniel Feingold

Daniel is a Barrister (Non-Practising) who heads Strategic Tax Planning, a Tax Law Consultancy that has as one of its specialities UK and International Tax Planning for both high net worth individuals and corporate clients. This includes both structuring for UK clients investing in property abroad and UK property acquisitions for foreign investors. His advice is sought after by many accounting and law firms around the UK and overseas.

Daniel has over 22 years experience specialising in tax law since qualifying as a Barrister in July 1983.

He has spent time at the Bar, in several leading City of London law firms and latterly in the International Tax Department of a leading accountancy firm, before establishing his own Tax Consultancy.

Daniel is the lead international tax expert and a technical author for www.property-tax-portal.co.uk.

Daniel has written and lectured extensively on property tax planning; including the pitfalls of Spanish and French property investment and is a regular contributor to several publications on the whole spectrum of tax planning, especially avoiding capital gains on property sales.

Daniel is known as a 'creative' tax expert and has formulated his own unique tax mitigating solutions.

You can learn more about Daniel on-line at the following link:

➔ **http://www.property-tax-portal.co.uk/consultancy_daniel.shtml**

19.2. Watch Out for the Single Solution Approach

The first and most important point to understand when considering overseas property investments is that one single solution will not fit all investment scenarios. This is regardless of what any advisor may tell you.

This is something that is very important (in fact critical) to understand.

You are likely to need an individual solution to fit around your specific circumstances and that is the key to successful tax planning in this area.

A solution that works for one person might actually trigger a huge extra UK tax liability for another.

19.3. Using an Offshore Company

One of the most popular solutions that is recommended time and time again for people who are investing in overseas property is to purchase the property through an offshore company.

This offshore company could be situated in country such a Jersey, Gibraltar, The Isle of Man or in fact, any well-known offshore tax haven.

The advisors who recommend such a structure usually claim that simply using such a Company will avoid the following taxes:

- avoid local capital gains tax
- reduce or eliminate local income tax
- avoid local inheritance laws and taxes
- avoid wealth taxes.

It is important to understand that most of these claims are not true!

19.4. The SEVEN pitfalls of using an Offshore Company

Below you will find the most common found issues with setting up and using an offshore company.

Income Tax on Rental Income
The one tax that the use of an offshore company will not reduce at all is the income tax on rental income.

This means that if the company that you have set-up receives rental income from your properties then local tax will be due on this.

Withholding Tax
It is also important to understand that most countries have what is called a withholding tax on rental income.

The agent or the tenant is normally obliged to deduct this tax and pay it over to the local tax authority. In practice, this sort of informal withholding is collected by the property owner having to pay the withholding tax over to the local tax authorities when filing their annual local tax return.

Another type of withholding tax is usually due, when you sell your property.

The property purchaser is obliged to withhold, 5% or 10% of the purchase price. This is handed directly over to the tax authorities in the country where the property is situated.

Examples of this include Spain where the purchaser must withhold 5% and the US where the purchaser must withhold 10% of the purchase price.

In both situations the only way to get the money back if your capital gains tax is less is to file a local tax return.

Offshore Companies do not avoid withholding taxes either on income or capital gains.

The other factor that is often missing in the advice that people are getting in these standard solutions is the UK tax perspective.

They can sometimes avoid Inheritance taxes.

The one tax they are usually good at avoiding is local wealth taxes, because these are applied only to individuals.

However the cost or running an Offshore Company is often as much as the annual wealth taxes!

Don't forget the UK Tax Perspective
It is all very well if your company can avoid local taxes supposedly, but you need to understand the UK tax law as well.

Offshore companies can create many UK tax problems – remember this!

There has been a long history of attack on the use of offshore companies. After all, if it was so simple to use offshore companies, then the use of onshore local standard UK companies wouldn't be such a regular occurrence!

The Anti-Avoidance Rule
When using an offshore company, it is also vital to understand that there is an anti-avoidance provision, which is now called section 739 of the Income and Corporation Taxes Act of 1988.

This is an anti-avoidance rule going back to 1936.

The objective of the rule is basically to look through any transaction where a person transfers their rights or their money to a person based outside the UK.

This can involve the transferring of rights or money to a company, trust or an individual with the objective of avoiding UK income tax.

This means that even if you set up an offshore company, then the rental income that is coming through that offshore company could still be taxable on you in the UK using this anti-avoidance rule and therefore be subject to UK income tax.

In other words, the offshore company will have no affect whatsoever for UK income tax purposes.

Charging of Capital Gains to Shareholder
There is also a parallel provision for capital gains tax that is section 13 of the Taxation of Chargeable Gains Act 1992.

This provision creates a "look through" if an offshore company sells a property for instance, and realizes a capital gain, and a UK shareholder has at least a 10% interest in that company.

The legislation will attribute a corresponding proportion of the capital gain the company makes to that individual. In other words, a "look-through".

Even if you simply put the shares in the name of your wife and your children, it will not work because the legislation will "look-through" that and charge the tax on you..

Every UK resident shareholder will end up getting a tax bill when the offshore company sells the property. The effect is there will be no tax benefits whatsoever for UK capital gains tax purposes from using an offshore company.

Benefits in Kind (BIK)
Another very real problem is a tax charge based on the use of the property, as a benefit in kind.

If you own your own UK Company then you may well already be familiar with this.

If the company provides you with a car then you pay tax based on the type of car that is provided by the company. This is a benefit in kind. If the company pays for the petrol that you use in the car, then again it is a benefit in kind and you are taxed on this.

The same thing happens with a property, if that property is used for your benefit.

If the property is a pure investment property and you rent it out then it is not a problem as you are not receiving any personal benefit from the property.

If you have an offshore company that is holding a property which you use as a holiday home then this will be treated as a benefit in kind and you will be liable to pay tax on this benefit. Even if you just use the property for two weeks in a year. Otherwise, you will have to pay tax on the benefit at your highest income tax rate.

Say that you own a holiday home through an offshore company in Portugal. In the summer months of August the rental income generated by this property would be approximately £2,000 per week.

Instead of letting the property out you decide to use it for a family holiday for two weeks. If you don't pay the company £4,000 then you could end up with tax bill of 41% on the £4,000. In certain circumstances, the benefit in kind charge can be higher than this, based on when the property is "available" (that is, not let to a third party), rather than when you actually occupy it.

Now it is not quite as simple as that, because the company also has to pay national insurance contributions at 12.8% on the benefit that you have received. If HMRC discover such a structure not declared to them and ask about personal use they may argue that it has been available all year to the tax payer. If the owner rents it out for some of the time and pays the BIK of his own accord on an ongoing basis, then this is unlikely to be raised. Even if it is raised HMRC will accept personal time use based on evidence. However if there is no evidence, then there will be a problem.

Please Note

In the 2007 Budget, it was announced that legislation would be introduced in the 2008 Finance Act to exempt the benefit in kind on a foreign property from tax, provided the following conditions are satisfied:

- The company owning the property is itself owned by individuals
- The property is the company's only or main asset
- The company's only activity is the holding of the property (it appears this exemption will only apply to one property)
- The acquisition of the property was not financed by a connected company

HMRC will be consulting on the details of this exemption, but where the above conditions are satisfied, they have said they will not seek to charge tax on this type of benefit in kind. This may help some investors, but the conditions above are likely to effectively exclude many property investors and only help holiday home owners.

Central Management & Control

Another very common and key problem with offshore companies is a concept of English tax law that is known as **central management and control**.

This is an approach that the HMRC are using more and more.

If an offshore company only has UK directors and it is run from the UK then HMRC will argue that the company's residence is actually in the UK for tax purposes. This is because its central management and control is in the UK and therefore it should be taxed like a UK company.

This means that if the company receives rental income then it will be charged to UK corporation tax.

There has been a case on this issue of company residence, the "Wood and another v Holden" case, which was decided on 26 January 2006 in the Court of Appeal in favour of the taxpayer. The HMRC have been refused leave to appeal the case to the House of Lords and are understood to be seeking another test case to take through the Courts.

The basis of this ruling shows that if a company is genuinely run from abroad then it will not be resident in the UK, but the strategies used by the company to achieve this are unlikely to be practical for the average property investor.

How to Avoid the Issue of Central Management & Control

In order for the problem of central management and control in the UK to be successfully avoided, the company would have to be run by directors who were not resident in the UK. These directors would then have to hold board meetings and make decisions about the company – and not just "rubber stamp" decisions made by the shareholders in the UK.

In other words, the company is genuinely going to have to be run outside the UK, presumably in the tax haven where it has been incorporated.

The real result of this is that it makes it very costly to operate an offshore company and another practical problem is that the investor loses direct control of his property investments because every time he wants to make a decision, he has to put that decision to the Board of Directors, who have to hold a meeting.

Therefore as you can imagine, it is not really very practical to achieve central management control abroad, although theoretically following the Wood and another v Holden case, it may be possible to do so.

19.5. Using Local Companies

An alternative strategy to using an offshore company is to use a local company in the place where the property is being purchased.

Now, sometimes there is a real need for this method in places such as Bulgaria where until a short time ago it was not possible for foreigners to own freehold Bulgarian property.

The only way to overcome this was to form a Bulgarian registered company, which could then hold the property.

Sometimes when you form a local company it can avoid the withholding tax rules on rental income and also reduce the amount of capital gains tax. However, although this is possible in practice it is not very common.

Challenges faced when using a Local company
Mostly local companies are taxed in a fairly similar way to any other individual holding property.

This means that once again you have got similar problems to running any offshore company from a UK perspective, as a result of the section 739 problem.

There is however a defence to this, which is to demonstrate that there was no tax avoidance motive. In other words, the reason for setting up the company was purely to comply with local property laws such as in the Bulgarian situation. If you can demonstrate this to the Inland Revenue, then it is possible that there will not be a problem.

However, it may be very costly in terms of professional fees, if HMRC takes up this point, to prove to them that your motive was not a tax avoidance one. So, in practice it may not be a desirable thing to do.

The other issue you need to overcome is section 13 of the Taxation of Chargeable Gains Act 1992.

19.6. Using a Double Tax Treaty to Your Advantage

Many of the double tax treaties between the UK and various other countries, for instance Bulgaria, Spain etc, will give one country sole taxing rights to a company's profits if a company is resident in that country.

In other words, the income passing through a local company holding investment property could possibly trigger a tax under section 739. The position on Section 739 and whether a treaty can protect against it is unclear! However, the good news is that a treaty will defend against capital gains tax being attributed to shareholders.

This therefore means that using a local company could prove a good way of creating a capital gains tax deferral.

Let us look at a practical example where this may happen.

Suppose you start off by purchasing a small apartment and after a few years you make a capital gain on it and you reinvest that money into larger villas. You will not create a UK capital gains liability at that point in the local company if the country where it is situated has a double tax treaty with the UK with the appropriate clause giving sole taxing rights to that country. However there may be local capital gains tax on the company.

Some countries have rules where if you reinvest the money in more property there is a deferral. This means that using a local company for reinvesting can create a successful deferral until you sell the shares in the company.

19.7. CM&C and Local Companies

Finally we come back to the issue of central management and control.

This can also be a problem with local companies, just as it is with offshore companies.

Therefore, to get the tax benefits of capital gains deferral and possible rental income deferral; you have to appoint local directors and make sure that they hold meetings. Once again there is a cost involved in doing this and therefore it is important to weigh up the costs of having local directors and meetings against the possibility of deferring capital gains tax and income tax.

19.8. Using a UK Company to Buy Overseas Property

Another solution available for purchasing property abroad is to actually use a UK company.

In this scenario the UK company will be set-up and managed in the UK and purchase properties overseas.

This is a good solution, if there are no **foreign branch** tax rules locally in the country where the property is situated.

19.9. Foreign Branch Tax Rules

Foreign branch tax rules can be triggered where a company is resident in one country, but is operating in another country. For example, you may own a UK company and use it to buy investment properties overseas and receive rental income from them. If that other country applies this "foreign branch" rule there could be tax due in that country on the profit made by the "foreign branch".

The country where the property is owned will charge the additional tax and this can in some cases end up being a major tax burden and problem.

If this is the case then using a UK company is not to be recommended.

Normally, however, the UK double taxation treaties such as those with Spain or Portugal will eliminate these foreign branch tax rules.

However, one place in which there is a particular problem with foreign branch tax rules is the United States. They will charge a foreign company operating in the US taxes of up to 39%.

Their corporation tax rate is approximately 34%.

They have a foreign branch tax, which is in fact reduced under the UK/US double tax treaty to 5%. When you add those together the cumulative rate is close to 39%, which is so high as to be prohibitive. This is especially so bearing in mind that a UK individual would only pay 40% capital gains tax on an investment and so using a UK company in the US is actually a disaster! (Because a UK investor then has to extract the money from the Company and face a further 25% on doing this by dividend.)

19.10. Associated Company Rules

You should also remember that the rules for "associated companies" described in section 3.2 above may mean that your investment company will be liable to UK corporation tax at more than 19% on its profits.

19.11. Understanding Foreign Tax Rates

Another thing to check is whether the local foreign taxes are higher than the 19% UK rate.

If your UK company tax rate is gong to be 19% and the foreign taxes are 25% then it is tax inefficient. Although you can set the foreign tax off against the UK tax, so you will not have to pay any UK tax, you cannot get a repayment of the foreign tax that is greater than your UK tax liability. This means that in this example you have lost 6% to foreign tax that you cannot recover.

19.12. Extracting Money from Your UK Company

We have already seen that if you pay income tax at the higher rate of 40%, you will have an additional tax liability of 25% when you extract dividends from your UK company.

19.13. Using Two Companies

A more complex tax solution that is sometimes recommended to people is to use a holding company to hold the shares in the property owning company. This will normally involve using both an offshore company and either a local or UK company.

The objective of this strategy is to sell shares in the local company or more often in the top company, which may be either a UK or an offshore company. In some situations this can prevent the capital gain on the sale of the shares in the property company being attributed to the UK shareholders of the holding company.

It is all very well for an advisor to recommend this solution, as it is good structure in certain situations can eliminate local capital gains tax.

However, one of the problems that I have come across is that when you come to sell your property you will find very few buyers who are willing to buy shares in an offshore or a UK company.

They just want to buy the property.

I have come across numerous instances where people have bought such structures and found out there are hidden tax liabilities.

These tax liabilities are in the country where the property is situated.

For a long time there was a structure whereby there was a Spanish company holding a property and above it was a company located in Gibraltar. Lots of UK individuals were encouraged to use this structure as a means of avoiding Spanish capital gains and wealth taxes.

In practice, most of these structures have turned out to produce hidden tax liabilities and the use of this type of structure has ended up not only costing a lot in tax, but also in professional fees to negotiate with the authorities to agree a settlement of the tax liabilities.

Portugal was one place where such structures were immensely common. However the Portuguese government introduced a special transfer tax at 16.25% to eliminate the advantages of such a structure. This means that anybody who is not aware of this and is offered a Portuguese property in a company could face a large tax bill there!

Most people are now aware of this. However if you are new to investing overseas and such a structure is offered then get proper professional advice.

I come across very; very few people who are prepared to take on these structures without doing extensive research and getting assurances from local advisors and UK advisors that there are no hidden liabilities.

On top of that the purchaser will want a substantial reduction in the price that they are paying for the property, just in case there are any hidden liabilities.

So the whole thing will end up being a very drawn out process and you will limit the number of potential purchasers to sell on to and you will end up taking a lower price.

So in reality, these double structure companies are generally to be avoided for the following reasons:

- They usually come with hidden taxes
- Two companies = two sets of costs of managing and running a company

- Few people are prepared to take on such structures, they just want the property
- Purchasing the structure can incur high fees as the purchaser will need to consult various advisors.

One final point that you must also not forget. If you have got an existing UK company then you could once again be affected by the associated company rules – see section 19.10.

19.14. Using a Nominee Company

This is a relatively new solution and can be useful in the right circumstances

The idea behind a UK nominee company is that it acts like a trustee. In other words, it is just holding the legal title to the property for the benefit of the beneficiary.

Normally that would be the purchaser - yourself.

The idea is that this UK structure relies on the fact that the foreign tax authorities do not understand this concept of English law, where you can separate out the legal title and the beneficial ownership. In other words, the name of the person registered as owning the property can be different to the owner in law. Most European countries do not have this concept although it tends to be used in some of the Caribbean countries.

If you can use this type of company it can be avoid local inheritance taxes, and possibly local capital gains taxes and wealth taxes.

However, it is highly specialized strategy and can only work in limited circumstances.

The idea that you can just pick one of these up off the shelf and use it to buy property anywhere would be misguided.

You need specific advice on how this is going to work for your circumstances and in the country where you are investing.

If this solution is available then it is a relatively cheap solution to implement.

19.15. FURBS

Finally I want to look at a very sophisticated idea that can be used as a way to hold foreign property investment.

This is a new opportunity that has opened up after April 6th 2006.

This solution is a **Funded Unapproved Retirement Benefit Scheme** or" FURBS".

It used to be possible to have a FURBS where the trustees were offshore. Previously if you put money into a FURBS from your own limited company then the money coming out of the company into the FURBS would qualify for a corporation tax deduction in the company.

But at the same time that payment would be treated as a benefit in kind and taxable on you at up to a 41% marginal rate.

For instance if you made a payment to a FURBS for £100,000, you would end up with a £41,000 tax liability.

Of course you have no money in your hands because £100,000 goes to the FURBS and so you would have to find the cash to pay the tax from elsewhere.

Now after April 6th 2006 the rules have changed.

The Company does not get a corporation tax deduction for the payment until you receive some sort of taxable benefit from the pension fund, which may be years in the future.

There is no tax liability on you for money taken out of your own company and put into an offshore FURBS.

This opens up the possibility of using an offshore FURBS as a holding vehicle for foreign investment property. It may need to use an offshore company to hold the property, but this is a genuine opportunity.

The way you can get money back from the FURBS is to treat it as a pension fund and eventually take out an annuity in the form of a guaranteed annual payment. This means you can either sell the property or take the accumulated rental income and that could be loaned back to you as one of the beneficiaries of the FURBS. You would have to pay the market rate of interest on that loan

Another way of actually getting money out of the FURBS is it can actually pay you all of the money that is in the FURBS but you will have to suffer UK income tax at 40%.

However, by having a very long-term deferral, in other words you might not make that payment until you're 65 or 75; you have built up a huge sum of money tax-free on an ongoing basis.

There may also be other methods of getting money out of a FURBS that are quite tax efficient. These involve the FURBS investing in special types of insurance bonds.

The important point to understand is that money can be extracted from the FURBS in tax efficient ways.

A FURBS is going to be quite costly to set up and there are going to be ongoing administration costs. However for a significant investment (say £1m plus property investment overseas) and for the right client it is a very useful tax deferral vehicle and one that clients in the right circumstances should really be looking at.

19.16. A Final Word

In this chapter I have covered off a number of solutions that may be proposed to you for investing overseas.

Some advisers will recommend 'off the shelf' packages to you that they will claim will mitigate taxes.

Being a specialist in offshore and International taxation and having worked in this area for over 22 years, it is my experience that too many of these 'off the shelf packages' will not work.

Every person who is looking to invest overseas will need specific tax advice based on their personal circumstances and their investment strategy.

So before you invest overseas, make sure you consult a credible international/offshore tax specialist.

Appendix A – Template Documents

On the following two pages you will find template documents that you can use.

Examples of these documents are given in section 6.4.

The two documents are as follows:

- Meeting Minute
- Dividend Voucher

Meeting Minute

Name of Company: ______________________
Company Registration No: ______________________

Address: ______________________

____

____

Minutes of a Meeting of the Board of Directors

Date of the meeting held at the Registered Office of the Company: ___/___/___

Present:

______________________ ______________________

______________________ ______________________

DIVIDENDS

It was resolved that the company pay an interim dividend in respect of the period ending

__/__/__ to holders registered as at __/__/__as follows:

Share Class	**Dividend Rate**	**Date to be Paid**
Ordinary of ________	________ per share	___/___/___

ANY OTHER BUSINESS:

____

____

Signed on Behalf of the Board

Name____________________ Date: ___/___/___ Position: __________

Dividend Voucher

Name of Company: ____________________
Company Registration No: ____________________

Address: ______________________________

____

Tax Voucher

Interim dividend for the period ending ___/___/___ to shareholders registered on ___/___/___

Payment Date
___/___/___

Shareholder Details
____
____
____
____

Shareholding	Dividend Rate	Dividend Payment	Tax Credit
______Ordinary shares of______	____ **per share**	**£**______	**£**______

This voucher should be kept. It will be accepted by HM Revenue & Customs as evidence of a tax credit.

____
(company secretary)

Date: ___/___/___

Appendix A – Case Studies

www.ingramcontent.com/pod-product-compliance
Ingram Content Group UK Ltd.
Pitfield, Milton Keynes, MK11 3LW, UK
UKHW051304110926
15112UKWH00019B/160

9 780955 574115